HANDMADE GARDEN PROJECTS

HANDMADE GARDEN PROJECTS

Step-by-Step Instructions for Creative Garden Features,
Containers, Lighting & More

By Lorene Edwards Forkner

Timber Press
Portland / London

Design by Patrick Nistler

Published in 2011 by Timber Press, Inc.

The Haseltine Building
133 S.W. Second Avenue, Suite 450
Portland, Oregon 97204-3527
timberpress.com

2 The Quadrant
135 Salusbury Road
London NW6 6RJ
timberpress.co.uk

Printed in China
Second printing 2012

Library of Congress Cataloging-in-Publication Data

Forkner, Lorene Edwards.
    Handmade garden projects : step-by-step instructions for creative garden features, containers, lighting & more / by Lorene Edwards Forkner. — 1st ed.
        p. cm.
    Includes bibliographical references and index.
    ISBN 978-1-60469-185-6
    1. Garden ornaments and furniture. 2. Do-it-yourself work. I. Title.
    SB473.5.F67 2011
    635—dc22   2011013136

A catalog record for this book is also available from the British Library.

To James, my partner in a handmade life

I'm a handmade gardening gal—
part eco-friendly, non-traditionalist, part
crafty creative with more ideas than money.
My garden is my canvas, my vision, and
my voice. A place where I am free of all rules,
except those of Nature herself. It's where
I make my unique mark on the world.

As kids we did this intuitively. My friends and I dug holes and pinched herbs from the neighbor's garden for imaginary feasts of chives and rhubarb. We carved trails in the blackberry underbrush and wrecked a fair amount of havoc on the landscape; did you ever make confetti from the stripped leaves of a cotoneaster? Works great! Pleasantly tired, thoroughly filthy, and completely blissed out, we fought off the dusk and parental calls to come indoors at the end of the day for a bath and bed. Begging for just a few more minutes, we could hardly bear to tear ourselves away from our muddy adventures—even if it was just until morning when we tumbled outdoors again, ready for another day of discovery.

Fast-forward to today. Somewhere along the garden path, outdoor fun and games have been hijacked by yard work. Demanding work schedules and responsibilities barely leave time for weekend mowing and blowing; boring, tedious, onerous jobs more like dusting and vacuuming than play.

Or, maybe you're like me: I fell for gardening—*hard*—with a passion known only to the truly plant-obsessed. From antique sweet peas to heirloom bulbs and the latest, greatest annual, I wanted them all. For thirteen years I was the owner and operator of a small specialty nursery called Fremont Gardens; a great way to scratch my acquisitive itch. What's more, I live in the Pacific Northwest, land of fertile soil, a benign climate, and more horticultural heroes and zealots than you can shake a hard-to-find, double-flowered, winter-blooming hellebore at. I was in good company and we reveled in a veritable horticultural heyday—until the weight of our garden chores nearly killed us.

There's far more to gardening than purchasing plants and following the latest design trend.

When was the last time you just goofed off in the garden; lolled in long grass or played house outdoors? Now that you're finally old enough to stay up past dark, why not watch the moon rise and witness the mysterious nighttime garden as it comes alive with heady fragrance, powdery moths, and unfamiliar noises?

I hope that this book—part idea inspiration and part instructional DIY guide—motivates you to get outside and craft your own personal landscape. You'll find a collection of clever, easy-to-make projects that convert basic hardware store materials, found objects, and the occasional bit of basement debris into distinctive garden furnishings with a modern sensibility and resourceful spirit. Craftsmanship and the expected level of construction expertise definitely fall on the make-do/can-do end of the spectrum with no sacrifice in the sophistication of the final result.

You might be surprised to discover that the first section—"Getting Started"—includes an exhortation to clean the garage. While that may not sound very playful, with a little indoor digging you may discover that you already own a great deal of everyday goods, scraps, and raw materials just waiting to be recycled, repurposed, re-envisioned, and imaginatively put to use in the garden.

Starting with the very foundation of your landscape, chapter 1 spotlights projects that accessorize and ornament pathways, patios, and even the lawn. Chapters 2 and 3 look at design and decor features that focus the eye and make up the heart of the garden with gathering spaces and creature comforts. Clever containers and stylish finishing touches—chapters 4 and 5—take your yard way beyond uniformity to a beautiful, one-of-a-kind space that's abundantly productive, comfortable, and entertaining. To help you manage the garden with style and efficiency, chapter 6 includes projects, tips, and practices focused on organization and storage.

Crafting projects with made-from-scratch ingenuity is easy, thrifty, and as much fun as those carefree days of yesteryear (and not nearly so hard on the cotoneaster). These days I cultivate a delicious vegetable garden where ornamental grasses and highbrow perennials once ruled. Overcrowded shrub borders have been supplanted by a generous fire circle and a tiny wooden deck furnished with a handmade cocktail table. Though my yard is still filled with lush plantings, it's no longer a tiger I have loosely by the tail. Today my garden fits my life and I'm having a blast.

Whether you have acres of land, a simple city-sized lot, an apartment balcony, or even just a somewhat sunny windowsill, I'll show you how to transform your little patch of the big outdoors into a refreshing, unique garden paradise.

Go outside—it's a nice day!

Acknowledgments

It is always a privilege to visit private gardens. I am especially grateful to Kathy and Ed Fries, Betty and Bob Hawkins, Johanna and Richard Marquis, and Sylvia Matlock and Ross Johnson for allowing me access to explore and photograph their very handmade landscapes.

At the heart of crafting is an adventure for experimentation and learning new things. Many thanks to Chris and Kristi Edwards who generously let me experiment with turf tattoos on their gorgeous lawn, and to Kathy Fries and Alejandro Gamundi for showing me how to transform humble wire fencing into seemingly intricate wire plant supports.

Juree Sondker at Timber Press has been my editorial guiding light and champion throughout the development and writing of this book; easily my biggest and most ambitious craft project to date. Heartfelt thanks to my loving friends and family for believing in me.

Finally, you would not be holding this book today without the constant and unwavering support of my husband, James, with whom I share a *very* handmade life; he cooked, he cleaned, he cheered, and he comforted me through the hard parts. We have a saying in our household: "don't push the river, it flows by itself." Honey, you were my lifeboat when the water got rough—thank you.

A street side freestanding doorway with a salvaged industrial metal entry floor is your first clue that the home and garden beyond are something special. Garden of Sylvia Matlock and Ross Johnson.

Getting Started

Handmade gardens are more than simply a collection of plants. Furnished with unique accessories, compelling features, and attention to detail, these personality-infused outdoor spaces embrace function and practicality alongside beauty and relaxation. As unique as a fingerprint and as distinctive as my voice or yours, handmade gardens reveal the creative vision and personality of the gardener in charge. Whether you cultivate rambling cottage-style beds and borders, maintain clipped modern formalism, or tend to a tiny terrace crowded with containers, dare to transcend off-the-shelf merchandise or somebody else's idea of style, and craft an environment filled with character, comfort, and fun.

Inspiration is everywhere. Personally, I prefer browsing the displays of many contemporary retailers for their clever styling ideas and subtle wit, than actually shopping the merchandise itself. Wander the aisles of home and hardware stores. From big box warehouses to tiny corner emporiums, you'll find a world of everyday materials and affordable goods waiting to be fashioned into one-of-a kind projects. Stone and lumber suppliers stock a wide variety of landscape materials from gravel mulch and rock to wood and metal fencing—the makings of distinctive garden furnishings with a modern sensibility and resourceful spirit. Architectural and industrial salvage yards, thrift stores, and the occasional dumpster hold treasure just waiting to be unearthed and repurposed.

Garden tours, flower shows, even a leisurely stroll through an unfamiliar neighborhood, can lead to garden discoveries and horticultural moments of inspiration. Books like this one, the vast internet marketplace and platform, as well as chatting over the fence with other inventive gardeners provide new ideas and backyard brainstorms. Best of all, the natural world presents us with a daily harvest of fresh designs and brilliant solutions if we only remember to keep our eyes wide and our minds open.

ECO-FRIENDLY SALVAGING AND REPURPOSING

It might seem strange to begin by cleaning out the garage, but often that uniquely American repository for all sorts of debris will yield miscellaneous basement flotsam and storage shed refuse which can be put to good use. One of the most eco-friendly moves we can make is to salvage and repurpose materials that would otherwise end up in a landfill.

Should you find yourself without a basement, storage locker, shed, or even a junk drawer to sift through, ask friends and family if you might have a go at their dark and tangled corners; they're bound to be thrilled at the offer. Neighborhood garage sales are an absolute treasure trove of just the sort of materials I'm talking about at rock-bottom prices, if not free. While you're at it, check out online listings and freecycle sites.

For larger quantities, and a potential bonanza of recycled riches, check out your local building salvage yard. In many large cities resourceful good folks are making it their business to salvage, sort, and retail used building materials and fixtures, keeping valuable goods out of the trash while preserving a little bit of history and a great deal of personality in the process. They do the heavy lifting and dirty work for us and it's worth every dime.

Explore the flexibility and functionality of a broad range of materials others might discard by employing an inventive spirit and utilizing a little creative re-vision. You'll save a ton of money and other natural resources making clever use of what is already right at hand.

A Closer Look—
THREE INSPIRATIONAL GARDENS

All gardens have the potential to be as unique and individual as the gardeners who craft them. The three extraordinary landscapes profiled in this section are particularly packed with inspiring ideas and imaginative solutions. Under the vision of their creative owners, everyday garden features and accessories become personal expressions of delight and a celebration of the natural world.

JOHANNA NITZKE MARQUIS is a gardener and an assemblage artist. Working in mixed media, her layered paintings, collages, and sculptures celebrate nature's intricacy, seasonal events, and minute exquisite detail. Her husband, renowned glass artist and collector extraordinaire Richard Marquis, is her creative partner and garden collaborator. Visiting their garden, located in a clearing at the heart of a mostly forested, 10-acre property on Whidbey Island in Puget Sound, I think I know how Alice felt as she tumbled down the rabbit hole.

True to the vision of the creators of this magical environment, the storied landscape invites close exploration. At every turn found objects and art, displayed in orderly multiples and carefully curated vignettes, mix with robust plantings. Colorful vines tangle with climbing roses above vegetable beds and perennials blooming with wanton abandon. Masses of casually reseeding annuals insinuate themselves into every nook and cranny in a riot of color. The property pulses with blossom and birdsong.

Enormous glass vegetables bedded down in a repurposed satellite dish form a fantastic installation greeting visitors at the entrance to the garden. Root Soup, 2008, mixed media, 8 feet in diameter, blown by Richard Marquis and crew.

Old fashioned climbing nasturtiums and sweet peas clamber up a pair of wooden ladders turned garden structure in the Marquis garden.

A signature combination of clipped formality, collector plants, chickens, and whimsy make up the delightful Fries garden.

A pirate's lair tree house complete with real buried treasure in the sandy "beach": high seas adventure among towering Douglas firs (Pseudotsuga menziesii).

KATHY FRIES is a passionate plants-person without an ounce of horticultural snobbery. Her garden, a narrow sliver of property 880 feet long by only 30 feet wide in places, drops steeply to the shore of Lake Washington; a layout that would make most professional garden designers turn in their drafting pencil and trowel. Yet since 1995, Kathy and her husband, Ed, have been transforming the once-bramble-choked hillside into a series of interlocking stylish garden spaces infused with wit and horticultural wonder. Brimming with an impressive collection of species rhododendrons, rare ferns, hydrangeas, and other shade-loving plants capable of instilling a serious case of plant lust, the landscape is also home to numerous found objects, quirky outbuildings, and handmade details.

Kathy is devoted to the notion of raising curious kids engaged with the great outdoors. Her two lucky boys, Xander and Jasper, graze their way through the productive vegetable garden, collect fresh eggs from the chicken coop, and plunder the high seas of their imagination in their very own pirate's den tree house. A new mountain bike circuit complete with thrilling dips and jumps, encircles Kathy's latest project, a stumpery. Gnarled root wads and downed timber harmonize with unusual cultivars and particularly choice selections of northwest native plants to create an understory garden in the shade of a second-growth forest. Play areas and gardens, chickens and clipped formality; just like Kathy, the resulting landscape is a blend of lighthearted whimsy and serious commitment.

A rustic chainsaw chair crafted from a downed fir is perfectly at home surrounded by formal details in the Fries garden.

Upholstered with moss, giant slabs of basalt form a monumental but comfortable bench in the woodland gardens of Sylvia Matlock and Ross Johnson.

SYLVIA MATLOCK AND ROSS JOHNSON are creative garden visionaries and owners of Dig Floral & Garden, a destination nursery located on Vashon Island in Puget Sound. I always come away from visits with an infusion of inspiration after perusing their collection of repurposed objects, clever container plantings, and hip hardscaping ideas, all of which complement their beautifully grown and displayed plants.

Ross and Sylvia, husband and wife as well as business partners, have a unique home garden that beats with a modernist's heart, an environmentalist's ethos, and a resourceful knack. Just like at the nursery, the couple has made brilliant use of repurposed and salvaged industrial materials; their contemporary home lives much larger than its tiny 700 square footprint might suggest. A mild-mannered maritime climate and a passion for their intensively planted garden prompted their decision to blur the line between indoors and out with glass walls that open accordion-style, inviting in the landscape.

Outdoor "decking" is actually a repurposed metal welding table used in shipyard and metal fabrication shops. The burnished patina echoes the warm-colored gravel and the russet trunks of the native madrones (Arbutus menziesii) in the garden.

Stacked giant catch basins form a bold retaining wall, introducing pleasing curves among the angular lines of the tiny contemporary home nestled in the trees on a high bank waterfront property above Puget Sound. Garden of Sylvia Matlock and Ross Johnson.

MY FOLLY

~~~~~~~~~~~~~~~

Traditionally defined, a garden folly is a fanciful outbuilding serving primarily as a design feature and foil for plantings. Indeed, folly may also connote an impetuous impulse, reckless whim, or wild hair. The purchase of my 1961 'Lil Loafer vintage trailer fits the bill on all fronts.

Never intended for travel, my little "canned ham" beauty sits in the back corner of the garden anchoring what I call my Aluminum Garden, surrounded by plantings of silver, green and white, and twilight purple. Instilling an expansive sense of destination even on my small city lot, my garden folly travel trailer—tricked out with roadmaps of my favorite destinations, cozy lighting, and comfortable benches—extends garden living well beyond the end of our growing season.

~~~~~~~~~~~~~~~

What's Your
FAVORITE OUTDOOR SETTING?

We all respond to gardens through the lens of personal experience and most people naturally gravitate to certain landscapes. Me? I love the beach and wide open spaces. I've used concrete rubble and rounded stones throughout my western Washington state garden, just off the coast of Puget Sound, to suggest a rocky Northwest beach. Glass and metal objects bring to my beachcomber's mind debris left on the shore after a good storm. I may not be able to afford waterfront property, but by evoking the spirit of a coastal landscape—waving grasses, reflective surfaces, and plenty of sky—I've created my own little beach house garden, without the taxes!

What about you? Maybe you enjoy hiking rocky trails and exploring alpine meadows filled with blooms; a landscape that embodies a beautiful contradiction of rugged and delicate. An intricate tapestry of groundcovers furnished with craggy boulders and dwarf conifers on an open sunny site brings that mountaintop experience into your city garden. After all, the somewhat harsh concrete canyons of an urban environment and the conditions on a windswept condo rooftop aren't so very different from those of an alpine peak.

Identifying the nature of a much-loved destination or space will help you kick-start the re-visioning process and begin to recognize materials you find intriguing. You'll be that much closer to creating a personal landscape that feels familiar, comfortable, and feeds your spirit at the same time as it meets your everyday needs. And you'll only have to duck out the back door to be in your favorite place.

A honeysuckle-scented sheltered nook offers refuge from the afternoon sun and a cushioned chaise for a well-deserved nap, reward for a productive weeding session. Garden of Johanna and Richard Marquis.

CREATE A GARDEN THAT FITS YOUR LIFE

Define goals for your outdoor space, focus on making them happen, and even the tiniest garden lives large. Ask yourself some questions to get started.

1. What do you want to do in your garden? Grow cut flowers and food? Entertain? Escape?

2. When are you available? If you work full time and are only free to spend time outdoors on weekends and in the evening, plan accordingly.

3. Do you prefer open, exposed space or enclosed, sheltered areas? A smart design can protect you from the heat of the day as well as nosy neighbors.

4. Ever heard the saying, "Mother Nature bats last?" Gardeners rarely win in the long run when trying to cheat climatic conditions (such as hardiness zone and soil type) so make sure to plan and plant for your garden's unique setting.

5. How do you access entrances, the driveway or garage, and any utility spaces? Design for comfort and practicality as well as aesthetics. An inviting entrance is important, but don't forget to leave room on either side of the driveway to actually get out of the car, or include a path so you can get the garbage out for Monday's pickup.

Gallery
OF MATERIALS

Plumbing pipe, vintage galvanized wire fencing, and buckets add gleam to garden projects.

None of the materials we'll be working with in this book are particularly exotic. In fact, most are readily available at neighborhood hardware and home warehouse stores—and I'm always astounded at what turns up in the basement! As you review the list, think about what materials best express your garden personality. Gather and organize, sort and separate. I find it helpful to divide my loot into several categories.

- **Wood.** Leftover lumber, unused shelving, discarded tables, broken furniture, sticks, bamboo, logs, bark, pine cones, arborist chips, cardboard, and newspaper.

- **Metal.** Galvanized buckets, plumbing pipe, rusty metal bits, wire, food grade cans, rebar, wire fencing, agricultural stock tanks, chain, and the occasional piece of sheet metal, tin, or copper.

- **Plastic, glass, stone, and soft materials.** PVC pipe and plastic containers, concrete, gravel, rock, shells, tumbled glass and pottery, glass bottles and jars, canvas, sheeting, burlap, old toweling, plastic tarps, bits of rope, and other miscellaneous objects.

Vintage croquet mallets and an old tennis racket lend personality to a wood-centric collection.

*Found objects and
quirky collections—
from bottle caps
to antlers—provide
finishing touches.*

BUILDING TOOLS

While sorting, clearing, and taking stock of your raw materials, make an inventory of tools and other supplies you already have kicking around. Fewer adaptable, multi-purpose, solid, well-crafted tools are far better than a collection of every doohickey and gizmo on the hardware shelf. Kit out a tool box with these suggested tools and supplies and you'll be prepared to tackle any project in this book; aprons and tool belts are optional—but do you really want to pass up the opportunity to don one?

- **Power tools.** Handheld power drill, electric chop box, and circular saw.

- **Hand tools.** Hand saw, rubber mallet, hammer, screwdriver, tin snips, wire and bolt cutters, pliers, needle-nose pliers, and builder's level.

- **Handy helpmates and other supplies.** Nails, wire, screws, measuring tape, clamps, sandpaper, zip ties, bungee cords, hooks, binder clips, duct tape, pencils, Sharpie pens, extension cords, heavy-duty construction adhesive, scissors, plastic tarp, whisk broom, dust pan, and step ladder.

Before I begin a project, I like to sort my tools and supplies into separate shoe box–sized plastic bins. That way, rather than carting my entire tool box around, I can organize what I need before hand and don't have to work around or sort through tools I'm not using. Of course, the trick is to return everything to its rightful place when the job is complete so you'll know just where to find those precious needle-nose pliers or the $1/2$-inch drill bit the next time you need it.

SAFETY FIRST

Sharp blades, moving parts, pointy objects, rust, and harmful dust all present potential health risks. Follow basic workshop good sense and most important of all, don't rush. Work with a sense of patience and keep alert to the task at hand.

- Create a well-lit, uncluttered work space before you begin any building project.

- Gather and organize your supplies and materials and check all power tools for intact electrical cords and solid connections.

- Wear close-fitting, protective clothing; avoid loose ties or dangling cords which might become dangerously entangled.

- Use eye protection as needed and wear durable close-toed shoes. (You can pick peas in flip flops but don't try to build in them.) Ear plugs will protect your hearing if you'll be working with power tools for an extended period of time.

- Utilize a simple, well-fitted, disposable dust mask to keep from inhaling harmful dust and irritating particles.

- Always wear gloves when handling solvent-based liquids and glues. I keep a box of lightweight latex gloves in the appropriate size with my tools.

- Keep a first aid kit nearby stocked with Band-Aids, sterile cotton, and antibacterial gel or wipes. It's also a good idea to stay up to date with your tetanus boosters.

The GROUND FLOOR

Wherever you garden, the horizontal surface—
the literal ground on which you stand—is
the perfect, if not somewhat obvious, starting
place to begin making a garden. It is on
this level that you'll carve out planting beds
and lay paths, dividing the area to create
your vision for the garden. The ground surface
not only determines the size of your garden,
but how you treat it greatly sets the tone for
the character of the space. Regional influences
reflected in your choice of materials ground
your landscape firmly in place—or indulge
in some environmental fantasy and evoke a
favorite distant locale.

Place a long-lasting, unique mark on your space by elevating hardworking surfaces—like a permeable gravel pathway or patio—to exciting ground treatments with decorative insets, custom pavers, or mosaic ornaments. But don't let fears of commitment keep you from experimenting and having some fun. Flirt with a temporary turf tattoo that's only as lasting as your mowing schedule allows. Or fashion a portable bamboo edging panel that can be easily moved around the garden to frame seasonal highlights, accentuate the curve of a pathway, or contain a billowing late season herb garden.

Bluestone-Quilted

GRAVEL PATHWAY

Eco-friendly gravel is the quickest and most economical way to lay a durable pathway or patio. Once laid, upgrade your hardworking but humble garden flooring with an arrangement of bluestone pavers set into the gravel. The cool color of the stone echoes the basalt gravel while veins of rusty brown add a touch of warm color. In my backyard, bluestone pavers mark the transition from gravel pathway to wooden deck like a Stone Age welcome mat.

Gravel is graded by the size of its rock particles and may or may not contain fines, or stone dust, which help create a firm, solid base. Washed gravels have had the fines removed. Larger sizes ($5/8$- to $3/4$-inch) are suitable for heavy-traffic areas like driveways or for building a sub-base. Finer grades ($1/4$- to $3/8$-inch) lend a more finished effect; use this grade for pathways, patios, and to top-dress deeper beds laid with a sub-base. Steer clear of pea gravel unless you like the feeling of trying to walk on ever-shifting ball bearings. Consult with your supplier or use an online calculator to figure how much material is needed for adequate coverage.

Purchase bluestone pavers at stone yards, or at home goods warehouses or garden centers that carry landscape building supplies—generally referred to as hardscape materials. Or you might approach friends or neighbors who are laying a patio to see if they have a few extra pieces. Most tools needed for this project are of the standard garden variety with the exception of a tamper, a weighted plate at the end of a long vertical handle that makes short work of firming up a newly laid gravel surface. Most large hardware stores and tool rental agencies have tampers available on an hourly basis.

MATERIALS

- Plastic edging material, stones, or recycled concrete
- Gravel
- 5 to 7 irregularly shaped bluestone pavers
- 2 (10-inch) rebar stakes (optional)
- Scotch moss (*Sagina subulata*)

TOOLS & OTHER SUPPLIES

- Shovel
- Wheelbarrow
- Fixed metal rake
- Tamper
- Small trowel
- Rubber mallet

INSTRUCTIONS

➡ **1. Prepare base.** Use a shovel to dig out your pathway or patio; the correct depth depends on your climate. In regions that routinely receive hard freezes, prepare a base at least 4 to 6 inches deep to accommodate soil shifting. In milder regions, excavating a base 2 to 3 inches deep is sufficient.

➡ **2. Set edging.** Create a boundary to keep gravel from shifting from your pathway into neighboring planting beds. Install rolled plastic edging material according to package instructions. Or, set rocks or chunks of recycled concrete at the perimeter of your prepared pathway or patio.

➡ **3. Lay gravel.** Haul gravel by wheelbarrow, dumping roughly consistent mounds throughout the space to evenly distribute the material. Rake gravel smooth and tamp firmly, locking the rough edges into an even, stable surface.

Shovel, haul, and dump gravel.

Rake and tamp gravel.

➡ **4. Determine composition.** Select an area of your gravel pathway or patio to highlight and accent with bluestone pavers. Set pavers on the gravel surface, trying out different arrangements until you come up with a pleasing pattern. The crazy quilt design pictured on page 42 measures just 18 x 36 inches.

5. Set bluestone pavers.
Excavate gravel with
a small trowel setting each
stone in place and leaving
a narrow channel between
each paver. Bluestone
pavers vary in thickness,
requiring you to adjust how
deep you dig the gravel to
end up with an even top
surface. Try setting one
small stone vertically for
a linear accent (as seen in
photo, right).

Laying out pavers.

6. Finish. Fill in gaps between set pavers with gravel, then thump
each stone with a rubber mallet to set them securely. Because
gravel shifts over time, you may need to hold pavers in place if your
finished composition is not on a completely level surface. To do so,
drive two 10-inch rebar stakes into the ground on the downhill edge.
A quick spray from the hose cleans the stones and settles the dust.
Plant quickly establishing Scotch moss in the gravel to soften hard
edges and link the finished pathway with adjacent plantings.

TRY THIS

A *Place pavers to mark the entry to your property or to highlight a spot where two paths cross.*

B *Substitute recycled chunks of broken concrete—sometimes referred to as "urbanite"— for bluestone pavers. Many salvage yards and recycling centers offer this material absolutely free for the hauling.*

PERMEABLE PAVING

Let's put water back into the soil where it belongs. Permeable or porous surfaces, like a gravel path or patio, allow rainfall and irrigation to percolate into the ground rather than spill into the street. Excess runoff sluicing over paved surfaces carries landscape chemicals and road gunk into the sewer system creating an enormous burden for municipal waste management agencies and the resulting toxic soup threatens fish and wildlife that populate our waterways and shorelines.

You can also search out affordable, creative, and locally sourced alternatives to gravel. In coastal regions you'll find crushed seashells. And in many cities, stone yards and landscape material suppliers stock crushed recycled concrete or brick. Here are even more permeable options for furnishing your garden's floor:

- Beach stones
- Broken and tumbled pottery or terracotta
- Decomposed granite
- Hazelnut shells
- Pine needles
- Recycled glass cullet
- Wood chips

URBAN COWGIRL PAVERS

Put a skip in your step and a shine on your spurs with custom pavers featuring a lucky horseshoe and old cast iron stove grates which, to my eyes, appear more like a brand than a discard from an obsolete appliance. Whether your pathway is cobbled with stone, brick, or pre-cast concrete stepping stones, adding these unique elements lends style and yippee-ki-ay personality to the most pedestrian walkways.

In order to remove isolated pavers, your existing pathway must be dry laid, that is, set in sand or soil not fixed in concrete. Find cast iron stove grates at salvage yards and used-appliance stores; lucky horseshoes have to find you. Sixty pounds is far more dry mortar mix than you'll need for this project. Keep the open bag of leftover mix tightly sealed and dry to prevent mortar from setting up and going to waste. Or put the extra to use crafting pebbly mosaic accents (see page 51).

MATERIALS

- [ ] Dry-laid paved pathway; my pathway is made up of 7 x 9-inch concrete pavers set in sand

- [ ] 1 bag (60 pound) dry mix mortar, a blend of sand and cement

- [ ] 3 cast iron stove grates, 8-inch diameter (or size that will fit in the space left by removed pavers)

- [ ] 1 horseshoe, 6-inch diameter

INSTRUCTIONS

➧ **1. Determine placement.** Arrange stove grates on existing pavers until you come up with a pleasing composition.

➧ **2. Remove pavers**. Pry up selected pavers using a sturdy screwdriver or strong trowel. Remove any loose soil or sand.

(continued)

Remove paver and confirm that the stove grate will fit in the empty space.

TOOLS & OTHER SUPPLIES

- [ ] Screwdriver or trowel
- [ ] Scrap of wood
- [ ] Tarp

Fill void with dry mix mortar.

➡ **3. Add mortar.** Completely fill empty spaces where pavers were removed with dry mortar mix. Use a scrap of wood to level mortar flush with the surrounding paved surface.

➡ **4. Set inset pieces.** Lightly sprinkle mortar-filled pavers with water from the hose until thoroughly dampened; use a gentle spray to keep from displacing dry mix. Allow excess water to drain. Firmly press horseshoe and stove grates (face down) into the dampened mortar.

➡ **5. Finish.** Cover finished pavers with a tarp and leave to cure for one week. Avoid walking on your new custom pavers until they are completely cured.

A   *Incorporate durable, weather-resistant materials like marbles, tile, and tumbled glass into your pavers for added color and excitement.*

B   *Experiment with other salvaged materials: the grill from a metal heating vent, sections of metal or PVC pipes, and even toolbox castoffs or old keys.*

C   *Press retired metal cookie cutters flush with the surface of dampened mortar for subtle but tidy outlines of various shapes, figures, numbers, or letters.*

Johanna and Richard Marquis's oversized garden monogram, crafted from bits of colorful glass and marbles and set into the poured concrete floor of a garden shelter, brands the space uniquely their own.

- -

Pebbly
MOSAIC PATIO ACCENTS

Mosaic accents lend pizzazz and a focal point to a serviceable but ho-hum gravel patio. A limited palette of mostly white, smooth pebbles set within repurposed metal hoops subtly suggest the ridges of an oyster's shell or the swirling movement of water. Similar stones may be purchased at florists, garden centers, or stone yards where you'll find a full spectrum of colors—warm terracotta-colored sandstone, beautiful blue-green pebbles from Mexican beaches, or moody jet-black stones. Or maybe just put that rock collection you've been gathering for years to good use.

For my mosaic forms I used a discarded 24-inch hoop from an old barbeque, a barrel stave 20 inches in diameter, and a scrap of metal pipe about 10 inches in diameter. You'll need about 100 stones (roughly 2 to 3 inches in diameter) for every square foot of your finished mosaic. See "Custom Shapes With Cardboard Forms" for instructions on making temporary forms.

Plan your project for a dry day and work shielded from direct sun as the mortar will begin to set up and harden once it is exposed to air and moisture. Only work as big a surface as you can complete in one hour; however, working in stages, you could turn your entire gravel pathway or patio into a series of brilliant, show-stopping garden mosaics.

- -

MATERIALS

- Smooth, rounded pebbles in a variety of sizes
- 3 circular metal forms, 1½ to 2 inches deep
- 1 bag (60 pound) dry mix mortar, a blend of sand and cement

INSTRUCTIONS

➡ **1. Determine placement**. Lay out your forms in different arrangements on top of the gravel surface until you come up with a composition that fills the space and complements the surrounding garden.

(continued)

- Trowel
- Builder's level
- 10-inch scrap 1x2 lumber
- Tarp

Arranging forms.

➡ 2. Build a working palette.
Take the time to organize and sort pebbles by size and color. This allows you to work more freely once you begin to lay out your design without having to stop and look for just the right stone.

Stones are sorted and ready to go.

➡ 3. Set forms. With a hand trowel, remove and set aside gravel that falls within each shape. Set the round forms into the gravel and firmly tamp the interior area to create a compact base. Use a builder's level to make sure your forms are even from side to side and sit flush with the surrounding gravel surface.

➡ 4. Create mosaic. Fill each form with dry mortar mix. Level the surface of the mortar with a scrap of wood, creating a sandy bed into which you will place your pebbles. Set pebbles vertically and snug with each other, ensuring that pebbles are at least halfway buried into the mortar mix; add or remove mortar as needed to completely fill the form. Only work one form at a time so the mortar doesn't begin to set up before completing your design. Create interest by contrasting size and color, placing pebbles in a way to suggest movement and repetition. As you're working, periodically tap the top of your mosaic with a scrap of wood to keep the surface even. Repeat with your other forms.

➡ **5. Finish.** Spray your finished work with water from the hose to activate the mortar and begin the hardening process. Use a gentle spray to keep from displacing the mortar and pebbles. Cover mosaics with a tarp and leave to cure for one week. Avoid walking on mosaics until they are completely cured.

Setting stones in the dry mortar mix.

TRY THIS

- -

(A) *Don't limit yourself to gravel surfaces. Create a beautiful focal point by placing a mosaic medallion at the center of your lawn. Or replace tired, well-trod turf with an exciting pathway of mosaic stepping stones.*

(B) *Preserve a memory of a trip to the beach or summer vacation by incorporating shells, trinkets, or other bits of suitably resilient ephemera. A wonderful project for kids and their parents— or grandparents!*

CUSTOM SHAPES WITH CARDBOARD FORMS

Maybe you don't want a metal outline for your finished mosaic— or maybe you don't have a stash of old barrels and barbeques waiting to be dismantled and repurposed. Disposable, temporary forms are an easy-to-make substitute. What's more, their flexibility allows you to make mosaics in any shape you can think of and fashion from cardboard.

Gather heavy-duty boxes from the liquor or grocery store, then take a sharp utility knife and carefully cut the boxes into 2-inch-wide strips. Join strips together with masking tape forming a narrow band long enough to completely define the outline of your finished mosaic. Set your temporary form following the instructions in step 3 of "Pebbly Mosaic Patio Accents" and continue through step 5. After curing your mosaic for one week, use a trowel to carefully remove surrounding gravel and peel or cut away the cardboard form. Backfill and tamp gravel firmly into place around your finished piece.

TEMPORARY TURF TATTOO

America's love affair with the lawn has waned in recent years, but among some its heart still beats strongly. Declare your affection for your yard (or send a message to loved ones) with a 6-foot heart temporary turf tattoo. All you need is a can of field-marking chalk and roughly 100 square feet of open lawn. Sure, you could freehand a design, but these simple directions yield sophisticated results—more handmade valentine than garden graffiti.

Spray-on marking chalk is typically used for striping athletic fields or laying out landscape projects. Aerosol cans, designed to dispense in an inverted position, cleanly mark precise lines giving you control over your finished design. Purchase water-based, field-marking chalk at large home goods and sporting supply stores, as well as through online vendors. The environmentally friendly, non-toxic formula won't harm turf or nearby plantings and is easy to remove from hard surfaces. Temporary turf tattoos last up to two weeks or until the next mowing.

MATERIALS

- Lawn, an area roughly 10 x 10 feet

- 1 bag (2 dry quarts) washed white sand

- 1 can water-based, spray-on, field-marking or landscape chalk

INSTRUCTIONS

➧ **1. Stake pattern.** Measure and mark with stakes and string, two 6-foot lines perpendicular to one another, intersecting at their midpoint. Connect all four end points with string to make a diamond shape.

➧ **2. Outline pattern**. Empty bag of dry, washed white sand into the plastic pitcher. Carefully following your outline string, dribble sand from the pitcher in a fine line, clearly defining the diamond shape.

➧ **3. Add curves to pattern.** Divide top left and right quadrants of your diamond placing a stake at each midpoint, 2 feet down on either side from the top point; we'll call these points "L" and "R" respectively. Create a simple compass by attaching stakes to both ends of a 2-foot length of string. Place one stake of your 2-foot

(continued)

- Measuring tape
- 6 marking stakes
- String
- 1 (½-gallon) plastic pitcher
- Lawn rake or push broom

marker at "L" and beginning at the top point of the diamond and holding the string taut, walk out a half circle finishing up at the left point of your diamond; dribble a little sand to mark the line. Repeat this procedure placing your string and marker compass at "R" to form the opposite curve of the heart. Remove all stakes and string.

String and washed white sand mark out pattern on lawn.

➧ **4. Tattoo turf.** Spray heart pattern with field-marking chalk following the outermost sand outline, disregarding interior reference lines.

➧ **5. Finish**. Allow ten to fifteen minutes for chalk to completely dry before "erasing" unnecessary lines by raking or sweeping sand into the lawn.

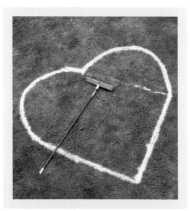

A sturdy push broom erases guidelines after marking.

A *Assert your love in living color. Floral spray paint in a broad range of colors may be purchased from craft stores and wholesale floral supply houses; non-toxic after drying.*

B *Take your message to the street, sidewalk, or playground—but be prepared to clean up after yourself by scrubbing with a sturdy push broom and water.*

MOW A MARK — WHY SHOULD GROUNDSKEEPERS HAVE ALL THE FUN?

Gardeners not ready to tag their turf can still put some fun into the relentless chore of mowing the lawn. Anyone watching a televised baseball game taking place at an outdoor stadium has no doubt marveled at the intricate patterns that appear on the field. At least this is the sort of thing I notice during an endless game of America's favorite pastime. Skilled groundskeepers, equipped with specialized mowing equipment, have perfected the art of mowing stripes, logos, and other designs into their turf, raising the tedium of mowing the lawn to an art form.

Specialized books, websites, and trade articles, solely dedicated to details of specialized equipment, benders bars, refracted light, and optimized viewing points, divulge turf design secrets for weekend lawn artists with big league aspirations. The rest of us are content with quick and easy effects:

• Mow a crisply defined pathway winding through a slightly shabby lawn to a distant corner of the garden creating an intriguing sense of destination or directing visitors to a bench in the shade.

• Draw attention to passing seasonal highlights, like a stand of sunflowers, or lead the way to the backyard party by mowing a simple arrow or exclamation point into the turf.

• Take a turn at lawn striping; all you need is a mower with a full width roller bar. Prepare your yard for a work of art by letting the lawn grow a little longer than usual and set your mowing blades higher than normal; short grass is hard to flatten sufficiently to create contrast. Visible lines result from mowing the grass directionally, appearing light or dark depending on the viewing angle. The pattern is most dramatic when seen from above, with many effects nearly invisible from the side.

A GARDEN JOURNEY

〜〜〜〜〜

Distilled down to a single element, this mown grass labyrinth creates a soulful garden of peace and contemplation on Vashon Island. Bob and Betty Hawkins created their labyrinth in 2000, siting it in a rough meadow at the top of a knoll above their apple orchard, overlooking nearby Puget Sound. The design follows the ancient seven circuit seed pattern and walking its 276-foot-long pathway is a part of their daily lives. The Hawkins, who travel the world visiting ancient and contemporary labyrinths, have helped to design and install several local labyrinths and facilitate tours of these unique public and private spaces on the island.

〜〜〜〜〜

Portable
BAMBOO EDGING

Ornament and detail your garden where pathway meets planting bed. This flexible 3-foot panel of wired together, irregular lengths of rustic bamboo is easy to construct and move about the garden defining, restraining, or simply framing seasonal effects. Unfinished bamboo beautifully complements naturalistic, meadow-like gardens filled with ornamental grasses and blowsy late season perennials, as well as appearing perfectly at home in pared-down, minimalist environments with open space and limited plantings.

Mature bamboo is a grass with the strength of wood and is naturally resistant to rot and pest infestation. Bamboo is one of the fastest growing plants in the world and is quickly becoming a valuable renewable resource, finding its way into every aspect of the construction, textile, and paper industries. Beautiful, lightweight, resilient, and easy to work, bamboo is an ideal material for earth-friendly gardens.

Sturdy bamboo poles are readily available at garden centers and hardware stores in many lengths and gauges. Cut poles to size quickly and cleanly with an electric chop saw. A hand saw, while effective, is harder to control on the hard, slick surface of cured bamboo, making dangerous slips of the blade more likely.

MATERIALS

- 5 (8 foot x ¾-inch) bamboo poles
- 14 gauge galvanized wire

INSTRUCTIONS

➧ **1. Cut bamboo.** Measure and cut bamboo poles into thirty-three 10- to 12-inch long lengths. Cut two 24-inch lengths from remaining bamboo.

(continued)

- Measuring tape
- Electric chop saw
- Handheld power drill, ³/₈-inch bit
- Scrap wood and nails
- Wire cutters
- Needle-nose pliers

▶ **2. Drill poles**. Drill each of the thirty-three shorter poles all the way through, 2 inches up from the bottom. Nailing a scrap of wood to the surface of your work space creates a fixed edge for lining up the ends of your bamboo, making this process easier and more accurate. Drill each pole a second time, 8 inches up from the bottom.

A scrap of wood nailed temporarily in place speeds drilling and accuracy

▶ **3. Thread poles on wire.** Cut two 40-inch lengths of 14 gauge galvanized wire. Working one drilled pole at a time, thread one wire through the bottom hole and the other wire through the top hole. Repeat with remaining drilled poles, adding them one by one to the parallel lengths of wire. Keep the orientation of each pole consistent for an even bottom edge; top edge will be uneven due to differing pole lengths. Distribute drilled poles along the wires spacing each piece of bamboo about ¼ inch from the next.

▶ **4. Form end stakes.** Drill remaining 24-inch-long poles at 10 inches and 16 inches up from the bottom. Keeping the top and bottom orientation the same as your already threaded poles, add these pieces onto wires at both ends of your bamboo edging. These end stakes will anchor the panel in the garden.

Thread the 24-inch bamboo poles on last, one at each end.

➡ **5. Finish.** Trim extra wire extending from each end of your edging panel to roughly 2 inches. Use the needle-nose pliers to coil each trimmed wire; this secures bamboo poles in place and creates a finished end.

Coiled wire keeps threaded bamboo intact.

TRY THIS

- -

A *Encircle a container planting of textural ornamental grasses with bamboo edging for a sleekly modern composition with Asian flair.*

B *Create a stylish but simple outdoor mat perfect for the porch, a greenhouse interior, or the floor of your backyard shower by wiring fourteen equal 36-inch lengths of bamboo together*

A delightful collection of old shovel heads has been artfully put to use edging a perennial border. The bronze tones of peony foliage go beautifully with the metal's patina. Garden of Johanna and Richard Marquis.

A modern alternative to the common lawn, sweeping groundcovers of dwarf ornamental grasses and grasslike plants carpet the garden with a soft surface in pleasing contrast to paved areas and hardscape features. Finely textured leaves animate the landscape, capturing movement and light, while a resilient nature and variety of growing habits provide lasting, year-round garden impact with minimal upkeep.

Grasses Beyond Turf

BLUE FESCUE
(Festuca glauca)

Steely blue mounding clumps of narrow foliage grow 6 to 10 inches tall. Provide full sun to part shade; tolerant of drought, heat, and poor soil.
EVERGREEN, ZONES 4–8.

BLUE OAT GRASS
(Helictotrichon sempervirens)

Blue-grey stiff, upright mounding clumps grow to 24 inches tall with flower spikes reaching 4 feet in summer. Provide full sun and well-drained soil.
EVERGREEN, ZONES 4–8.

DWARF FOUNTAIN GRASS
(Pennisetum alopecuroides 'Little Bunny')

Uniform compact clumps of dark green foliage sport buff-colored plumes in late summer before turning golden russet in fall; grows 10 to 12 inches tall. Provide full sun to light shade, moderately drought tolerant once established.
DECIDUOUS, ZONES 5–9.

DWARF LILY TURF
(Ophiopogon japonicus 'Nanus')

Handsome dark green grasslike foliage grows 4 to 6 inches tall in dense mats for a beautiful lawn substitute. Provide evenly moist soil in partial shade.
EVERGREEN, ZONES 6–10.

JAPANESE FOREST GRASS
(Hakonechloa macra)

Lush green weeping mounds of graceful leaves grow to 24 inches tall. Provide partial to bright open shade and an evenly moist soil. Variegated forms (H. macra 'Albostriata' and H. macra 'Aureola') light up shady conditions with cream and green or gold and green foliage respectively.
DECIDUOUS, ZONES 5–9.

MEXICAN FEATHER GRASS
(Nassella tenuissima)

Silky blond tresses on this softly tufted grass grow 12 to 24 inches tall, waving and whispering in the slightest breeze. Provide full sun to light shade and well-drained soil; weed out unwanted seedlings.
EVERGREEN, ZONES 7–11.

ORANGE SEDGE
(Carex testacea)

Fine blades of copper-brown have orange tips that become more pronounced in winter. Not a true grass, this gracefully mounding perennial grows 12 to 18 inches tall. Provide full sun to part shade and evenly moist soil.
EVERGREEN, ZONES 6–11.

TUFTED HAIR GRASS
(Deschampsia cespitosa)

Verdant green clumps grow to 15 inches tall, profusely flowering in early summer with light and airy panicles that rise to 3 feet. Provide partial shade and evenly moist soil, foliage holds up best where temperatures are moderate.
EVERGREEN, ZONES 4–8.

VARIEGATED JAPANESE SWEET FLAG
(Acorus gramineus 'Ogon')

Striped golden yellow and green foliage grows 10 to 12 inches tall in a neat, tidy mound. These grasslike plants tolerate light foot traffic emitting a sweet scent when trod upon. Provide sun to shade and evenly moist soil; will tolerate boggy conditions.
EVERGREEN, ZONES 6–8.

SUPPORTING ACTS

Any heartfelt passion has its control issues and gardening is no exception. Nurseries and garden centers stock elaborate devices for staking, tying up plants, trussing tomatoes, and restraining plant growth. But put these gadgets in place when they should be—that is, well before plants burst into growth—and the garden quickly starts looking like a scantily clad pretty girl wearing only foundation garments; it's hard to see anything but the support.

Luckily, the projects in this chapter attractively stake, prop, and gently guide plants without stealing the spotlight from the beautiful garden starlets they support. Scrap metal brings a surprisingly organic quality to a rugged trellis and a durable planting ledge; an obelisk of lashed-together natural bamboo poles lend architectural substance to airy grasses and clambering vines; and humble hardware store wire fencing artfully transforms into a delicate sculpture that can hold its own on any garden stage. For an encore, these simple structures provide valuable vertical growing space for plants that might otherwise smother the ground and steal the scene.

Rugged
STEEL TRELLIS

Appearing elegantly organic and almost woven in texture, my rugged steel trellis is actually a scrap of industrial waste. Incredibly strong, virtually indestructible, and beautiful besides, rock screen scrap is my favorite heavy metal. Slotted between a couple of substantial shingled pillars, the rock screen offers a scaffold for clambering vines while discreetly screening an under-deck service area where I stash my wheelbarrow and wind the hose. The heft of the salvaged material balances the scale of the pillars while the rusty finish is a warm contrast to the weathered siding and echoes bronze-colored plantings throughout the front garden.

Rock screen—sometimes referred to as rock separator or rock grizzly—is an industrial material designed to sift and grade different sizes of rock and gravel. It's available in a variety of weights, from the brawny 3-by-3-inch grid used in this project down to a fine $3/4$-inch mesh. Scraps are generally priced at less than a dollar per pound at my local industrial salvage yard. You'll have to contact an industrial metal supplier about sourcing new material. Unless your salvage yard can custom cut pieces to size, it's best to keep an open mind, scouting for interesting pieces and suitable weights. I let the pieces I find dictate their use; this weighty piece is perfect for a trellis but requires heavy-duty bolts and a sturdy overhead beam to soundly secure it.

MATERIALS

- 1 piece heavy gauge rock screen; mine is 15 x 54 inches with a 3-inch grid
- 2 heavy-duty 4-inch hex bolts, $1/2$-inch diameter

INSTRUCTIONS

➡ **1. Position trellis.** Measure rock screen grid and determine spacing for bolts so the top of your trellis hangs level and with its weight evenly distributed. Drill pilot holes for bolts 8 to 10 inches apart. Using wrench, tighten bolts, securely anchoring them 2 inches into the supporting beam with the remaining 2 inches and head of each bolt sticking out.

(continued)

- Measuring tape
- Handheld power drill, ³/₈-inch bit
- Adjustable crescent wrench or ¹/₂-inch ratcheting socket wrench

Sturdy bolts anchor into a substantial beam.

▶ **2. Finish.** Lift and mount rock screen onto the protruding bolts. It's a good idea to have someone help you place the heavy trellis. Sow seeds or transplant vines and train them up the trellis.

Skip the heavy lifting altogether. Train plants up a rock screen trellis leaning against a sturdy fence or wall.

B *Replace a section of solid fencing with a framed piece of lighter weight rock screen. This window or porthole aperture offers a peek-a-boo view into the landscape beyond and introduces interesting patterns of shadow and light.*

TYPES OF TRELLIS

A trellis can be any two-dimensional, openwork panel that provides a vertical surface for growing plants. Freestanding trellis panels partition the garden into rooms within the larger landscape, delineating without completely dividing. Whether that space is a convivial dining area for twelve or a private corner for reading with just enough room for one, the semi-transparent nature of a trellis—as opposed to a more solid fence or wall—ensures you are never completely cut off from the rest of the garden.

On a more practical note, a trellis panel can direct foot traffic or simply screen the trash. Wall-mounted trellises supporting a tracery of vines or pruned woody shrubs relieve the expanse of a long fence or break up an empty façade—a living wallpaper.

Your choice of trellis material is another opportunity to highlight the unique character of your garden's setting. A prim and proper wooden lattice smartly finished in gloss white paint connotes elegant formality and conservative estates; the same panel left unpainted, grayed with weather, and draped in a blossoming profusion of climbing roses brings to mind casual seaside cottages.

Freeform structures more casually woven from willow, dogwood, or split bark have traditionally held a sort of storybook temperament. But the same materials in the hands of today's visionary landscape artists yield organic, wild, and wooly structures that appear animate. Indeed, crafted from freshly cut willow whips, these structures readily root, becoming a living sculpture of wood and green shoots.

Scrap Metal

WINDOW LEDGE

This airy planting ledge capitalizes on the handsome good looks and inherent strength of rock screen. Its delicate grid, greatly scaled down from other pieces in the garden, casts filigree patterns of light and shadow, while elevating a container chock-full of plants to the height of my kitchen window so I can enjoy the verdant view from inside or out.

My ledge is composed of two vintage, 9-inch metal shelf supports and a 7-by-34-inch scrap of rock screen. Keep your eyes open for rock screen scraps and end cuts when scouting metal and salvage yards. Regardless of how sturdy the rock screen and metal shelf supports are, your finished planting ledge will only support as much weight as your mounting hardware will bear. Choose appropriate masonry or wood screws to securely attach shelf supports to your exterior wall.

MATERIALS

- 2 metal shelf brackets sized to accommodate your rock screen ledge; mine are 9 inches long

- 1 piece lightweight rock screen, mine is 7 x 34 inches with a $1/2$-inch grid

INSTRUCTIONS

➡ **1. Determine placement.** Taking into account the depth of your planter, decide the height you want to hang your planting ledge. Measure and mark where shelf brackets will sit, placing them roughly 4 inches in from each end of the rock screen; my brackets sit roughly 26 inches apart. Using a builder's level, check to be sure your markings are even before drilling pilot holes for the mounting screws.

➡ **2. Mount brackets.** Screw the first shelf bracket in place, lining up pilot holes with mounting holes on the bracket. Repeat with the second bracket, again checking to be sure that your ledge will sit level before tightening screws securely.

(continued)

TOOLS & OTHER SUPPLIES

- [ ] Measuring tape
- [ ] Pencil
- [ ] Builder's level
- [ ] Handheld power drill and appropriate bit
- [ ] Mounting wood screws
- [ ] Screwdriver

Mounted metal brackets.

➡ **3. Finish.** Place rock screen scrap across mounted shelf brackets. Your planting ledge is now ready for its planter.

___

This quirky dragonfly with its 40-inch wingspan hangs on the side of our house. Northwest artist Kerry McGuire fashioned the durable sculpture from rock screen and other pieces of metal scrap.

TRY THIS

- -

 Load up a sunny back porch planting ledge with containers of fresh herbs and save yourself a trip to the garden every time you need a sprig of parsley or pinch of thyme.

Ⓑ *Pots of cheery, early spring flowers (such as miniature daffodils and grape hyacinths) lined up at window height bring the garden almost indoors, helping cooped up gardeners survive the last dark days of winter.*

 If you can't find a suitable scrap of rock screen, keep your eyes open at the scrapyard for metal wire kitchen shelving.

HOW TO RECYCLE
A DEAD TREE

Who says every tree needs
a root run? Kathy Fries
found a creative and
resourceful way to repurpose
a venerable but fading fruit
tree by chopping it down,
reducing it to its strongest
limbs, and inverting it over
a woodland pathway.
Securely anchored in place,
today her once-blighted
plum proudly stands as a
quirky arbor lending
character, vertical interest,
and a delightful story
unique to her garden and
resourceful vision.

Towering

BAMBOO OBELISK

This lashed-together bamboo structure provides a striking architectural focal point in the garden. Upright lines direct our vision prompting even the most ground-focused and planting-obsessed among us to pause long enough to take in the entirety of our garden's environment and include the sky in the composition. Enter the trellis, teepee, plant tower, or obelisk to provide vertical growing space for lush flowering vines and contain plants that might otherwise take over the garden.

Bamboo poles are strong, durable, sustainable, and possibly free if you have this attractive plant growing in your garden (see "Grow Your Own Bamboo Poles" for details about the harvesting process). Reasonably priced bamboo poles may be purchased at most garden centers and hardware stores in varying gauges and lengths. When selecting a location for your finished obelisk, consider sight lines, empty spots, and anywhere your garden could use an exclamation point—perhaps punctuating the end of a pathway or interrupting an expanse of evergreen hedging with a tower of colorful vines.

MATERIALS

- 6 (8 foot x ³/₄-inch) bamboo poles
- 8 (6 foot x ¹/₂-inch) bamboo poles
- 14-inch plastic zip ties

INSTRUCTIONS

➡ **1. Prepare poles.** Clear a workspace where you can lay your bamboo poles out on the ground; a driveway or level area of lawn or patio works well. Measure and cut four of the 8-foot bamboo poles to 6-foot lengths using the hand loppers. Cut the remaining two 8-foot poles into 2-foot lengths. You should now have four 6 foot x ³/₄-inch poles, twelve 2 foot x ³/₄-inch poles, and eight 6 foot x ¹/₂-inch poles.

(continued)

Bamboo poles cut to length.

2. Set base poles. Set the four 6 foot x ³/₄-inch bamboo poles in an 18-inch square using the rubber mallet to pound the poles at least 6 inches into the soil. Horizontally lash four 2-foot poles to the top of these uprights with zip ties to square off the structure. Repeat this procedure lashing another tier of 2-foot poles into position mid-structure.

3. Form structural X-shaped supports. On each side of the obelisk, drive a 6 foot x ¹/₂-inch pole into the ground to form a diagonal from the base of each main upright connecting to the top of an adjacent upright. Stabilize the cross-brace by lashing with zip ties at the point where the poles cross; secure with zip ties at the top and base of each upright. Repeat cross-braces on all four sides of the structure.

Zip tie connection.   *Crowning pyramid.*

4. Crown the obelisk. Create a decorative pyramid by lashing the remaining four 2 foot x ³/₄-inch poles to the top of each main upright. Gather the poles at the center, crisscrossing to form a tight bundle. Secure with zip ties cinching tightly to hold the resulting peak firmly in place.

5. Finish. Tighten zip ties to straighten and align all connections working from the top of your completed structure down. Snip loose tails on all zip ties for a tidy finish.

A   *Add a decorative element to your finished obelisk by wrapping the most visible zip tie junctures with copper wire. You can purchase copper wire or salvage it by stripping surplus electrical cable.*

B   *Go for an edgy industrial chic look and substitute iron rebar for bamboo when building garden structures.*

GROW YOUR OWN BAMBOO POLES

Harvesting poles from overgrown, possibly out-of-control bamboo yields generous quantities of this strong, flexible building material and transforms a congested clump into a pleasingly elegant and dramatic garden highlight.

To protect the health of your bamboo, never remove more than one-third of a clump each year and do not harvest new growth. Select individual stalks—botanically referred to as culms—that are at least two to three years old with fully matured "wood." Poles that are 1 to 2 inches in diameter at their base are best for most garden projects. Harvest at soil level using sharp loppers and a hefty dose of upper body strength. You may find a small folding pruning saw is easier to work with if the stand is especially crowded. Remove side branches from the main stalk with pruning shears.

Cut newly harvested poles to uniform lengths and grade by width. Stout, 2-inch diameter, 8-foot lengths make strong uprights. Bamboo poles with a 1-inch diameter can be used in a multitude of ways in the garden from crafting bean teepees and tomato towers to staking dahlias and marking rows in the vegetable patch. Slender whips are good for lashing projects and flexible enough to wind into graceful curves or weave between stronger elements.

Bamboo is characterized as either clumping or running, depending on its growth habit. Clumping bamboos expand in gradually increasing stands, sending underground stems or rhizomes out a few inches beyond the edge of the existing clump before sending up that year's crop of vertical woody shoots. Running bamboo can be alarmingly invasive, vigorously spreading by underground runners which shoot out to various, and sometimes great distances depending on the parent plant and environmental conditions, before sending up an annual crop of vertical shoots. Left uncontrolled, running bamboos quickly colonize the entire garden and your neighbor's garden as well. Be a good horticultural citizen and contain all running bamboo with a sturdy 24- to 30-inch deep root barrier of durable 30- to 60-mil plastic, sheet metal, or concrete.

Here are a few running bamboos that are particularly suitable for harvesting:

- Black bamboo
  (*Phyllostachys nigra*)
- Giant leaf bamboo
  (*Indocalamus tessellatus*)
- Golden bamboo
  (*Phyllostachys aurea*)
- Japanese arrow bamboo
  (*Pseudosasa japonica*)
- Square stem bamboo
  (*Chimonobambusa quadrangularis*)
- Temple bamboo
  (*Semiarundinaria fastuosa*)
- Timber bamboo
  (*Phyllostachys bambusoides*)

Galvanized
WIRE PLANT SUPPORT

With the intricacy of a spider web and the allure of lace, this sculptural plant support crafted from galvanized fencing elevates humble materials to high art. I appreciate these beautiful forms as much for their seemingly complicated and beautiful network of ripples and crimps as for the support they offer scrambling vines and billowing perennials.

Welded wire fencing may be purchased at the hardware store in 50-foot rolls that are 3 feet wide; enough material for several plant supports. Gather some friends for an afternoon craft session. Graceful curves emerge as crimping rows cinch the wire into an elegant form you'd never dream started with a roll of serviceable fencing. The trick to producing even results is to keep your twists uniform in placement and degree. The secret really is all in the wrist. With a little practice, standard pliers, and a bit of brute strength, you'll be stylishly managing plants and spinning garden magic in no time.

MATERIALS

- 1 roll welded wire utility fencing, 2 x 4-inch cell mesh

TOOLS & OTHER SUPPLIES

- Measuring tape
- Clothespins
- Bolt cutters
- Pliers

INSTRUCTIONS

➡ **1. Cut fencing**. Measure and cut roughly 4½ feet of welded wire fencing material from the roll, cutting down the middle of the nearest closed cell. Following the natural curl of the material, form fencing into a loose cylinder. Trim the first upright wire of every other closed cell starting at the top of the loose cylinder and working your way down along one cut edge. Repeat on the opposite cut edge, staggering the pattern so closed and open cells alternate opposite each other.

(continued)

Cutting pattern.

Fastening cylinder.

2. Form cylinder. Fasten one edge of your cylinder to the other by wrapping each extending horizontal wire around the opposite upright to tightly secure. Trim wrapped wires neatly. Push, prod, and gently manipulate the cylinder to form a uniform tube.

Crimping with pliers.

3. Crimp. Count down three rows from the top of your upright cylinder marking the bottom wire of the 2 x 4-inch cell with a clothespin to identify your first crimping row. Placing pliers firmly at the center of the first cell in the marked row, twist your wrist to the right at a roughly 45-degree angle to create a subtly crimped ripple in the wire. Continue working each cell in the marked row all the way around the cylinder. Moving up 1 cell toward the top of your cylinder, repeat this same twisting move, only this time twist your wrist a full 90 degrees to create a more pronounced crimped angle. As before, continue working each cell all the way around the upright cylinder.

4. Form top detail. Divide cylinder into four roughly equal sections around the top before proceeding to crimp the next row of wires. These sections will become petal shapes crowning your finished plant support. Place a clothespin marker at the side seam, then count how many cells make up the complete circumference and divide this number by four. My cylinder has 26 cells. Place a clothespin marking the top wire of the first cell to the right of the side seam. Count off the next 6 cells and place a clothespin on the top wire of the 7th cell. This time, count off the next 5 complete cells and place a clothespin marker on the top wire of the next cell, or the 6th cell following your last marker. Repeat the pattern counting off the next 6 cells and placing a marker on the top wire of the 7th cell, leaving you with 5 complete cells ending the row. Your pattern will look like this: clothespin–6 cells–clothespin–5 cells–clothespin–6 cells–clothespin–5 remaining cells. The slight inconsistency between the sections will not be noticeable in your finished piece. Remove each horizontal wire marked with a clothespin, cutting cleanly at each end using bolt cutters.

➡ **5. Final crimp.** Proceed with crimping the next tier of horizontal wires above your last crimped row, this time twisting your wrist and pliers beyond 90 degrees. Work the very top wire, your divided row, in the same way. Holding the pliers as before, twist your wrist as close to 180 degrees as possible; this should form a tightly stacked series of "S" curves. Work carefully to keep from popping the wire welds with these tight turns.

➡ **6. Finish.** Complete your plant support by rolling each of the top divided sections outward, splaying the curves into graceful petal shapes.

Dividing top cells

Finished wire support structure.

TRY THIS

A   *It really doesn't get much easier than this: forgo the crimping and simply form a length of lightweight galvanized or vintage hairpin wire fencing into a cylinder. Acting as an almost invisible armature for blooming vines or blowsy perennials and lax shrubs like heavy-headed blooming peonies and mophead hydrangeas, these subtle supports quietly allow the plant itself to shine.*

B   *While not as long-lived as a wire cage, a globe-like sphere woven of supple dogwood (Cornus) twigs and secured with zip ties and wire offers another support option. The pleasantly organic quality makes it appear to have sprung fully formed from a highly organized and helpful shrub in the garden.*

A plant support structure made of dogwood (Cornus) twigs is pleasing all on its own; later in the season a scrambling vine nearly obscures the support.

HANGING GALVANIZED GARDENS

Turn a sculptural plant support into a unique hanging basket with way more style—and strength—than standard off-the-shelf frames. Form a cylinder by following the "Galvanized Wire Plant Support" instructions through step 2. With bolt cutters, reduce the height of your cylinder to 12 inches by cutting the upright wires. This should yield a cylinder with finished, closed-celled edges on both ends.

Proceed with steps 3 through 6, crimping and forming the crowning petal shapes around the top rim. Then invert the frame so petals are facing down; what was once the base of the cylinder is now the top edge of your hanging basket frame. Enclose the bottom of your basket by securely attaching a scrap of $1/4$-inch wire hardware cloth over the opening between the four petal sections.

Pad the completed frame with a thick layer of sheet moss or a coir liner and plant with lush ferns. Hanging baskets can get quite heavy so be sure to suspend with sturdy wires and a strong anchoring hook.

Wire waves and curves repeat the graceful fronds of common rasp fern (Doodia media) for a hanging wire basket of uncommon beauty.

Easy to grow, lush foliage, bountiful blooms, and nearly instant impact all in a single growing season—what's not to like about flowering annual vines?

Flowering Annual Vines of Summer

CANARY CLIMBER
(Tropaeolum peregrinum)

Fluttery dark yellow flowers really do resemble little canaries clinging to stems clothed with serrated bright green leaves.

GROWS 8 TO 10 FEET IN PARTIAL SHADE TO FULL SUN.

CARDINAL CLIMBER OR HEARTS-AND-HONEY VINE
(Ipomoea xmultifida)

Tiny crimson trumpet flowers attract hummingbirds to this vigorous morning glory cousin.

GROWS 10 TO 20 FEET IN FULL SUN.

CLIMBING NASTURTIUMS
(Tropaeolum majus)

Funnel-shaped blooms in shades of orange, red, and yellow reliably swathe scrambling vines all summer long. Bonus: leaves and blossoms both have a peppery watercress flavor and are delicious in salads.

GROWS 6 TO 8 FEET IN PARTIAL SHADE TO FULL SUN.

CUP AND SAUCER VINE
(Cobaea scandens)

Pale creamy green flowers develop violet stripes on their way to becoming deep purple "cup and saucer" blooms.

GROWS 8 TO 12 FEET IN FULL SUN.

EXOTIC LOVE VINE OR SPANISH FLAG
(Ipomoea lobata)

Multicolored spikes of blossoms change in a rainbow-like progression from red to orange, yellow, and cream set off by deep green lobed leaves.

GROWS TO 15 FEET IN FULL SUN.

MORNING GLORY
(Ipomoea purpurea)

Saucer-shaped flowers the color of a summer sky are produced anew each morning on this old fashioned cottage garden favorite. (Not to be confused with nasty bindweed, a noxious weed.)

GROWS 8 TO 10 FEET IN FULL SUN.

PURPLE HYACINTH BEAN
(Dolichos lablab)

Large pendant racemes of purple or white flowers stand out from dusky, heart-shaped leaves followed by curious dark purple bean pods with a metallic sheen.

GROWS TO 10 FEET IN PARTIAL SHADE TO FULL SUN.

SCARLET RUNNER BEAN
(Phaseolus coccineus)

Brilliant sprays of scarlet blossoms, beloved by hummingbirds, are produced from mid-summer to frost on sturdy twining vines. Plump pods swell with "magic beans" beautifully marked with hot pink and black—possibly Jack's original beanstalk!

GROWS 10 TO 12 FEET (QUICKLY) IN FULL SUN.

FEATURE ATTRACTIONS

On certain days our backyards deliver something close to ecstasy: a rich concoction of visual delight, heady fragrance, tactile gifts, and sweet flavors. On others, the cacophony of power tools, blighted views, and parched exhaustion threatens to swallow us whole in a confused jumble of overwhelming stimuli. Focal points—such as a gathering spot or a decorative garden feature—highlight and concentrate our attention on the beautiful attributes of a landscape as they gently distract us from the less-than-positive aspects.

The delightful projects in this chapter offer both creature comforts and practical solutions, as good looking as they are hard working. A burbling fountain masks the rabble of the outside world and lures birds, butterflies, and other pollinators. The warmth of a blazing firepit and the congeniality of an outdoor cocktail table invite lounging and lingering long after the sun sets, extending garden life into the evening hours. And a plumbing pipe pergola is my lighthearted—and admittedly quirky—take on a historic garden classic. Whether drawing our eyes or engaging and soothing the rest of our senses, these features provide a comforting

Old World
WATER FOUNTAIN

Fashioned from a substantial water jar that looks like it belongs in a historic European landscape, this fountain lends rustic charm as well as an enchanting soundtrack to the garden. No plumbing skills required; just plug this self-contained water feature into an outdoor electrical source and quiet the noise of the outside world with a resonant and soothing cascade.

The larger your container, the deeper the resulting tone will be—think water trickling deep within a cavern. My lightweight metal plant stand is sturdy enough to support the glazed saucer but linear enough to not take up too much space within the pot which would deaden the acoustics of the finished fountain. You can find oversized glazed pots at some garden centers or large hardware stores. Small submersible pumps are available at garden centers in the water gardening department, well-stocked hardware stores, pet stores, and through online vendors. Be sure to locate your fountain within an extension cord's reach of an outdoor electrical outlet to bring power to your pump.

Select a durable, all-weather pot that will stand up to winter conditions in your garden or be prepared to disassemble the fountain each fall. In my Pacific Northwest garden, I leave my fountain running year round. Throughout our generally mild winters, the pump prevents the re-circulating water from freezing. It has successfully withstood fifteen winters and temperatures down to about 10 degrees F. If an extended deep freeze is expected, unplug the pump and bring it indoors to protect it. In seriously cold climates where below-freezing temperatures are the norm, empty the jar of water and place a lid over the opening to keep rain and snow from accumulating and possibly bursting the jar as the ice expands.

MATERIALS

- Concrete paver, mine is 12 x 12 inches; or a bucket of gravel

- Frost-safe, water-tight, glazed container; mine is 28 x 24 inches with an 18-inch diameter

- Metal plant stand; mine is 22 inches tall

- Glazed saucer, roughly 1-inch smaller than the opening of your container

- Submersible, re-circulating pump, 115 volt

- 3½ feet vinyl tubing, ⁵⁄₁₆-inch inside diameter

- Weighty decorative rock or chunks of glass

- Outdoor grade extension cord

TOOLS & OTHER SUPPLIES

- Scissors or tin snips

INSTRUCTIONS

➡ **1. Position water jar.** Place your container on a solid, level surface, either a concrete paver or a tamped-down bed of gravel.

Assembled components.

➡ **2. Place plant stand inside water jar.** The top of the metal plant stand should come to just beneath the rim of the water jar's opening. If necessary, add a layer of gravel to the bottom of the container raising the plant stand to the correct height. Once the plant stand is properly situated, fill the jar a quarter full with clean water.

➡ **3. Position pump.** Immerse one end of the vinyl tubing into a glass of hot water to soften the vinyl—this will make sure it forms a tight seal—before connecting the tubing to the outlet

Pump and tubing.

feed on your pump. Submerge the pump in the water jar but keep the electrical cord and the free end of the vinyl tubing hanging over the rim and outside the large container.

▶ **4. Finish assembly.** Rest the glazed saucer on the plant stand. Measure the vinyl tubing so it reaches up to and over the edge of the glazed saucer; trim excess tubing with scissors or tin snips. Anchor the vinyl tubing inside the saucer with stones, chunks of glass, or another weighty material.

▶ **5. Connect power.** Plug the power cord for the pump into an extension cord that runs to an outdoor electrical source. As the pump engages, it will draw water from the bottom of the jar up through the vinyl tube, filling the saucer. When the saucer overflows, the water cascading over its edges and back into the reservoir at the bottom of the jar will create a sonorous tone.

TRY THIS

Dial down the scale of your fountain. Use a smaller container and pump to create a table-top version that can be tucked into the corner of a small deck or patio.

SOUND IN THE GARDEN

What we hear has a tremendous impact on how we perceive a space. Loud or soft, fast or slow, constant or intermittent, sound is yet another way we can alter and manipulate our garden experience. Given the reality of our often crowded environment, noisy, raucous sounds—whether from annoying power tools, busy streets, or an alarming rooster—intrude on our space and ratchet our nerves, while the sound of moving water wraps us in a pleasing surround of soothing white noise.

Hard surfaces refract sound while soft ones absorb and muffle. Think of a bouncing basketball on the neighbor's driveway compared with the click of croquet balls over a cushy expanse of lawn. A sound in the near distance, such as the splash of a gentle fountain, masks and dulls the roar of traffic in the background creating a private space, seemingly far removed from the hustle and bustle of the outside world. Site a fountain at your entry and notice how street sounds fade away. Set your dreams to water music with a fountain placed just outside your bedroom window. Or freshen sun-baked outdoor living spaces with the splash of cooling waters.

Monumental sections of municipal catch basins make up the three tiers of this impressive fountain designed and installed by Ross Johnson at Dig Floral & Garden. The bold scale of the feature is appropriate to the large open space of the nursery yard and its raw form reads pleasingly modern.

Simple
BACKYARD FIREPIT

The garden is a different place after dark. Like the proverbial moth, folks can't help drawing together around a backyard bonfire for its warming blaze and satisfying whiffs of wood smoke. The drama of flickering flames and shifting shadows creates an environment completely removed from the familiarity of daylight while the heat of a fire extends outdoor living into the cooler months of the year.

   With a few simple materials and a healthy dose of fire safety common sense, you can be enjoying glowing embers and toasting your toes by sundown. The repurposed base of a kettle grill or a task-specific fire bowl predrilled with drainage holes, assures your firepit is nearly maintenance free, come rain or shine. Surrounding the pit with a gravel patio provides a fire-safe, level surface and is easily dug to accommodate the fire bowl. The stone-filled gabion benches encircling our firepit were professionally welded to our specifications; for more information on gabions see page 105.

MATERIALS

- 12 to 14 river rocks, 10- to 12-inch diameter
- ½ bag (½ cubic foot) coarse builder's sand
- Steel fire bowl or kettle grill base, 30-inch diameter

TOOLS & OTHER SUPPLIES

- Measuring tape
- Tarp
- Shovel

INSTRUCTIONS

➡ **1. Select a location.** Choose a spot for your firepit away from low-hanging overhead branches and adjacent combustible surfaces, like a wooden fence or deck, which an escaping spark might ignite. Clear away all brush and any dead or dry vegetation in at least a 10-foot circle around your proposed firepit site. It is critically important to provide enough room for people to safely move around the firepit without crowding or stumbling.

➡ **2. Create foundation.** Measure a 36-inch circle and outline with river rocks to form your firepit foundation. Lay out a tarp to facilitate cleanup. Using a shovel, dig a 10-inch deep hole within the rock circle; set aside removed gravel and any sub soil on your tarp. Fill the hole with about 4 inches of sand.

(continued)

FIRE SAFETY

A warm fire is beautiful and mesmerizing but safety should always be your primary concern when using your backyard firepit. Follow these sensible safety tips and never leave a fire unattended.

- Check with local authorities for any restrictions or burn bans in effect due to dry conditions or poor air quality. Also be sensitive to prevailing winds and avoid building fires that will smoke out the neighbors.

- Only build fires outdoors and in the open to prevent potentially dangerous fumes from accmulating in areas without adequate ventilation.

- When building your fire, start small using twigs, black and white newspaper, and scrap wood for kindling along with matches and natural wax-based fire starters. Avoid toxic chemical fire starters and never use a petroleum accelerant on an open flame. Dry-seasoned wood burns cleanly and is less likely to spit sparks than green or sappy wood.

- Do not build fires when conditions are windy. Sparks and embers can catch a breeze and travel great distances, igniting dry grasses, roof tops, and other vulnerable aspects of the landscape.

- Keep a fire extinguisher or a garden hose with a spray nozzle nearby to quickly and effectively smother escaping embers.

- Always extinguish fires completely at the end of the evening. Douse smoldering logs with water until steam no longer rises or smother the fire with sand.

Prepared base.

▶ **3. Set fire bowl.** Place your fire bowl onto the foundation and add more sand as necessary to form a secure, stable base. Pack river rocks in the circle with reserved gravel and extra sand until each rock is fixed firmly into place.

TRY THIS

Gardeners without an old kettle grill to disassemble or an actual fire bowl can purchase a reasonably priced commercial wok from a kitchen supply house. Fashioned from steel and oversized to handle restaurant volumes, an industrial strength wok stands up to heat and the elements. Bed into stones as previously outlined or look for an iron plant stand to support your wok-turned-fire bowl above a gravel or paved surface. Between bonfires, a plywood round from the hardware store keeps out rain and turns your firepit into a handy table.

CREATURE COMFORTS

Because there's more to life than garden parties, plan for outdoor private space as well. This salvaged cast iron tub sits in the far back corner of my garden, sheltered behind a stand of ornamental corn. Filled with water from the hose at the beginning of a day of garden chores, by late afternoon the water is warmed by the sun—perfect for a cooling, low-tech, soap-free plunge. Pull the plug and garden grime and cares of the day simply drain away; it's quite refreshing!

Gabion-Style
COCKTAIL TABLE

It's easy to create a swank surface for the evening cocktail hour—garden style—with a ring of wire fencing, a pile of rounded river rocks, and a repurposed glass top. My backyard lounge table, located where it gets afternoon shade and furnished with weathered but well-loved Adirondack chairs, is a wonderful place to sit back, relax, and toast the beauty of a summer sunset.

My table's wire base is fashioned from a scrap of vintage hairpin fencing that I salvaged from an abandoned garden in my neighborhood. I love the extra detail and character of its crimped and scalloped edge, which is easily seen through the clear glass top. This sort of vintage fencing can often be picked up for a song at garage and tag sales, however any sort of heavy-duty metal fencing may be used and is available by the roll at most hardware stores.

If your garden does not produce an annual harvest of stone, source 10- to 12-inch river rocks at stone yards or landscape materials supply yards. Safety tempered glass is best for outdoor applications. You can purchase ready-made glass tabletops at import stores or custom order through hardware stores and glass suppliers; I found my glass top at a yard sale. I recommend starting with your glass top and adapting the size of your rock base to fit. Directions are for a 24-inch square glass tabletop with rounded corners that sits on a base approximately 20 inches in diameter.

MATERIALS

- Heavy-duty, metal hairpin fencing, 18 x 60 inches

- 30 to 40 river rocks, 10- to 12-inch diameter

- Tempered glass tabletop

INSTRUCTIONS

➡ **1. Form wire cylinder.** Trim wire fencing to an 18 x 60-inch rectangle. If you are using hairpin fencing the scalloped edge will be the top of the table supporting the piece of glass. The opposite border—the bottom—should be clipped to a finished edge. Connect the vertical sides of the frame to form a cylinder by clipping wires and wrapping them around the opposite side; crimp with pliers to secure.

(continued)

- Bolt cutters
- Pliers

Hairpin fencing detail.

➡ 2. Position table. Set cylinder in place and fill the wire frame with river rocks. Place flat sides of stones so they sit flush to the walls of the wire frame. Arrange the top tier of stones to provide a level surface so your glass top rests securely on the wire rim of the frame.

Finished base.

A Skip the fencing altogether if you come across a sturdy metal basket. Simply fill with stones and top with glass for an instant table. Or cover with a cut-to-fit piece of plywood and a cushion for an outdoor ottoman that provides extra seating or a place to put your feet up.

B Crown a rusty metal urn with a glass top for a more refined table that's easily moved anywhere in the garden.

WELDED GABION STRUCTURES

Welded wire mesh boxes, cylinders, or baskets filled with stone, repurposed broken concrete, or "rip rap" are called gabions. An adaptable building method with roots in Ancient Egypt, today gabions are widely used in civil engineering projects to effectively and economically construct retaining walls and shore up waterside and highway embankments. Gabions scaled down to backyard dimensions make for stylish, economical, and sustainable garden walls, furnishings, and decorative structures. The straightforward materials required—standard wire concrete underlayment with 3-inch openings and smooth iron bar—are regular stock at most hardware stores, metal shops, and industrial scrap yards.

While actual welding is beyond the scope of most DIY garden crafters, finding someone to do the work for you is easier than you might think. Check with local community and technical college programs for students with access to tools and equipment looking for a class project. Auto body shops, metal artists, and scrap metal yards are other possibilities. If you really want to tackle the job yourself, sign up for a beginner-level metal working class through a local art school or metal fabricator. Search for resources online using key words: metal, welding, fabrication.

The gabion bench in our backyard is composed of five separate box-like modules that measure approximately 36 inches long by 18 inches wide by 18 inches deep. Open at the top and bottom, the boxes are really just bolted-together trapezoidal cages designed to hold the river rocks in place. They form a semi-circular seating

A welded column filled with river rocks in my front courtyard.

area that embraces our firepit while retaining a change of level in the back garden. The gabions are topped with 1-inch thick bluestone pavers measuring 18 by 24 inches to form a sturdy seating surface. The finished bench is structurally sound yet requires no additional foundation and if needed, could even be disassembled and moved. This serviceable utility—and beautiful appearance—come at a fraction of the cost of an actual stone retaining wall.

PLUMBING PIPE PERGOLA

Need an escape from nosy neighbors or the hot sun? A pergola—a series of linked together upright posts—furnishes an outdoor space with an implication of a roof, creating a sense of shelter and privacy. (First popular in formal gardens of the Italian Renaissance, pergolas offered courting couples a leafy escape from the disapproving eyes of family members crowding villa terraces overlooking the garden.) Because of its scale, a pergola is a powerful design element capable of visually and literally linking one part of the garden to another.

To complement my vintage aluminum travel trailer, I chose galvanized plumbing pipe when constructing my not-so-traditional pergola which spans an undersized, ground-level wooden deck. Lightweight wire cables strung between the uprights comprise the roof. Before the canopy of annual runner beans and climbing squash fills in, a quick and easy awning fashioned from a cotton canvas painting drop cloth protects us from the afternoon sun (see "An Almost Instant Awning" for more details). It's a spectacular place for whiling away a lazy afternoon in the shade.

This project is ambitious in its scope—far and away the most involved undertaking in this book. Grab a partner or two and have some fun. Most of the work can easily be accomplished over the course of a weekend, but keep in mind that a full week of drying time is required before the project can be completed. Composed of standard lengths of threaded plumbing pipe, once the right pieces have been gathered, the uprights are easily screwed together and attached to poured concrete fittings. You'll find the best selection of threaded plumbing pipe and joinings at large hardware stores where you'll also find bagged concrete, cardboard tubes, woven wire cable, and all the other materials needed for constructing your own horticultural iconoclast.

It is critical that all measurements spanned by pipes are accurate. Learn to love your measuring tape and builder's level. Galvanized pipes are rigid with little, if any, flex; an exceptional material for constructing a strong pergola, but not very forgiving if your measurements are off—unless a wonky circus fun house look is part of your grand plan. Distances spanned with wire are more flexible. My finished pergola measures 7 feet tall by 5 feet wide and spans about 10 feet.

MATERIALS

- 4 (4-foot) rebar stakes, $\frac{1}{2}$-inch diameter
- 4 (5 foot x 1-inch) galvanized pipes threaded on both ends (A)
- 4 (1-inch) galvanized couplings (B)
- 4 (1 x $\frac{3}{4}$-inch) galvanized reducing bushings (C)
- 4 (18 x $\frac{3}{4}$-inch) galvanized pipes threaded on both ends (D)
- 4 ($\frac{3}{4}$ x $\frac{3}{4}$ x $\frac{1}{2}$-inch) galvanized reducing "T" (E)
- 4 (2 x $\frac{3}{4}$-inch) galvanized nipples (F)
- 4 ($\frac{3}{4}$-inch) galvanized caps (G)
- 2 (5 foot x $\frac{1}{2}$-inch) galvanized pipes threaded on both ends (H)
- 1 (4 foot x 8-inch) cardboard tube
- 2 bags (60 pound) quick-setting concrete mix
- 4 (1-inch) galvanized floor flanges (I)
- 16 (3-inch) bolts
- 1 (24-foot) length woven wire cable, $\frac{3}{16}$-inch gauge
- 4 flush-type clamps for wire

TOOLS & OTHER SUPPLIES

- Rubber mallet
- Measuring tape
- String
- 4 (3-foot) bamboo stakes
- Hacksaw
- Posthole digger
- 1 (5-foot) board
- Builder's level
- Wheelbarrow or tub for mixing concrete
- Shovel for mixing concrete
- Wrench
- Bolt or wire cutters

INSTRUCTIONS

▶ **1. Establish pergola footprint.** Pound a 4-foot rebar stake securely into the ground with a rubber mallet. Measure a 5-foot span and drive another rebar stake into the ground to establish the position of one end of your pergola. Measure off the distance your pergola will span lengthwise and repeat this procedure to determine placement of the other span.

▶ **2. Finalize placement.** Connect the top of all four rebar stakes with string, measuring along their length to ensure your lines remain parallel and square.

3. Assemble plumbing pipe upright spans.
Fit together one of each of the first seven plumbing elements (A–G) connecting them in the order they are listed. Repeat to form all four upright legs of your pergola. Form spans by inserting one 5 foot x ½-inch threaded pipe (H) between a pair of uprights at reducing "T" (E); repeat assembly for the other end span. Hand-tighten all joins, but not too tightly, as you will be undoing them before final assembly.

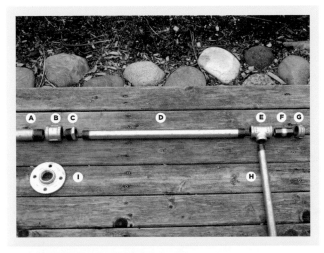

Plumbing pipe components.

4. Temporarily position upright spans.
Sleeve completed upright spans, which look like an upside down squared off "U," over the rebar stakes you laid out in step 1. Stand back and view the composition from various points in the garden to be sure you are satisfied with the alignment. A sound visual reading, where everything "looks right," makes more sense than careful calibration since lot lines, land contours, and adjacent plantings are usually not exactly in line either. When you are satisfied with final placement, disassemble 5-foot span (H) and set aside all upright pieces.

Remove rebar stakes and set aside, replacing them with bamboo stake placeholders. This is where you will pour the footings.

5. Prepare footings.
Cut cardboard tube into four 12-inch lengths with a hacksaw. (In colder climates footings should extend below the level to which the ground freezes.) Using a posthole digger, dig a 12-inch deep hole at each bamboo stake marker. Place cardboard forms into holes. Check that each end span form is level to its opposite by resting a 5-foot board across the tops of

the forms and checking with a builder's level; make necessary adjustments. Paired upright end spans, joined across the top by a pipe, must be level to fit properly.

Cut footing forms.

6. Set rebar in footings.
With cardboard forms in place, set the rebar that helps to firmly unite the uprights with their base. Using the rubber mallet, pound a 4-foot rebar stake straight into the center of each footing form to anchor securely. I have sandy soil and ended up driving the rebar about 6 to 8 inches into the soil, leaving a little less than 3 feet showing above the lip of the cardboard.

(continued)

7. Pour first two footings. Empty a bag of concrete mix into your wheelbarrow and slowly add water to the mix according to package directions. Stir the mixture with a shovel, adding more water as necessary until you have a thick pudding-like consistency. Divide wet concrete between the pair of cardboard forms taking care to keep the rebar stakes centered. Keep checking with the builder's level to ensure that the stakes remain plumb.

Completed footing.

8. Set first upright span. Allow concrete to set up for about twenty minutes so that the base of each upright won't completely sink into the wet mix. Thread a flange (I) onto the base of two pergola uprights. Reconnect a 5-foot span (H) between a pair of uprights. With each partner holding one side, sleeve this end span over a pair of rebar stakes, lowering it until each flange is firmly in contact with the wet cement. Concrete may seep up and over the anchoring flange; just make sure uprights remain perpendicular to the footing. Pound anchoring bolts into the wet cement through the four holes in each flange. You have about one hour to set your upright pipe pieces in their final position from the time you mix your concrete.

9. Set the other upright span. Repeat steps 7 and 8. With uprights in place, tighten all joins with a wrench to firm up connections.

10. Cure footings. Leave the freshly poured concrete with plumbing pipe uprights in place to dry and fully cure for one week before proceeding with the next step.

11. Connect upright spans. Cut two 12-foot lengths of woven wire cable. Form a loop by bending wire cable back on itself about 1 foot from the end and secure with wire flush clamp. Measure just over 10 feet from the tip of the loop and repeat to form another loop in the opposite end of the cable. Repeat this process on the second 12-foot length. Connect upright end spans by placing wire loops over the protruding caps (G) to form a slightly swagged wire span. If you would rather have a taut line, adjust clamps and tighten wires once wire loops are in place.

Wire loop detail.

12. Finish. Sow seeds or place transplants along the length of your finished pergola. Train vines on uprights and along wires as they grow to fill in a leafy canopy. Another option is to install a canvas awning to provide immediate shade.

TRY THIS

(A) *Don't stop there! Lucky gardeners with large gardens can extend the length of their pergola; just keep adding paired uprights joined with wire cable until you run out of room. Can't you just picture a plumbing pipe pergola running along a skinny corridor or side yard, crowned with a tangle of 'Heavenly Blue' morning glory? Glorious indeed.*

(B) *Go with the gleam of galvanized. Ordinary metal chain link—that most prosaic of garden fences—gains punchy attitude and verve backing up a plumbing pipe pergola.*

Scarlet runner beans and a string of Christmas lights festoon my late summer hideaway.

AN ALMOST INSTANT AWNING

Check out the painting supply aisle at the neighborhood hardware or home goods store for an unexpectedly fabulous, sewing-free awning for your finished plumbing pipe pergola— cotton canvas drop cloths. They come in a range of generous sizes, are easy to throw in the wash for cleaning, and are unbelievably affordable. (They also make great all-weather picnic blankets and tablecloths.)

I transformed a humble, 4-by-15-foot hall runner drop cloth into a casual awning that wards off the summer sun until my sowing of annual vines and climbing vegetables fills in. Grommets placed at either end of the runner and every 3 feet along its length allow it to be lashed with rope and hooked into place along the wires and over the loops of my pergola. An everything-included, easy-to-install, heavy-duty grommet kit from the hardware store and a rubber mallet made the process a breeze. Iron-on patches, available wherever sewing notions are sold, reinforce the canvas at each grommet to prevent tearing.

My finished awning can be adjusted to let in our sometimes shy Northwest sunshine, or removed entirely and stored for the winter.

Ahhhh—breathe in the heady perfume of a lily or the archetypal scent of a rose and we nearly swoon with pleasure. The smell of mountaintop conifers, the salty tang of the seashore, or the evocative aroma of a newly mown lawn has the power to deliver us back in time and space. Personal association and past experience build our memory bank of fragrance. It's a crying shame that our sense of smell diminishes as we age; perhaps it's an evolutionary parting gift that it lingers in our recall to be called forth with an unexpected whiff. Cultivate some sweet memories by working a few aromatic plants into your garden beds and containers.

Fragrant Plants

WOODY PLANTS

Citrus (*Citrus*)

Daphne (*Daphne*)

Lavender (*Lavandula*)

Lilac (*Syringa*)

Mock orange (*Philadelphus coronarius*)

Rose (*Rosa*)

Rosemary (*Rosmarinus*)

Sage (*Salvia*)

Star jasmine (*Trachelospermum jasminoides*)

Sweet box (*Sarcococca*)

Sweet gum (*Eucalyptus*)

Sweet olive (*Osmanthus*)

Viburnum (*Viburnum*)

Witch hazel (*Hamamelis*)

PERENNIALS

Bearded iris (*Iris germanica*)

Bee balm (*Monarda*)

Carnation (*Dianthus*)

Catmint (*Nepeta*)

Evening primrose (*Oenothera*)

Garden phlox (*Phlox paniculata*)

Honeysuckle (*Lonicera*)

Lily of the valley (*Convallaria majalis*)

Peony (*Paeonia*)

Sweet rocket (*Hesperis matronalis*)

Sweet violet (*Viola odorata*)

BULBS AND TUBERS

Daffodil (*Narcissus*)

Dwarf iris (*Iris reticulata*)

Freesia (*Freesia*)

Grape hyacinth (*Muscari*)

Hyacinth (*Hyacinthus*)

Lily (*Lilium*)

Peacock glad (*Gladiolus callianthus*)

Tuberose (*Polianthes tuberosa*)

ANNUALS AND TENDER PLANTS

Alyssum (*Lobularia maritima*)

Angel's trumpet (*Datura/Brugmansia*)

Annual phlox (*Phlox drummondii*)

Chocolate cosmos (*Cosmos atrosanguineus*)

Flowering tobacco (*Nicotiana*)

Four o'clock (*Mirabilis jalapa*)

Heliotrope (*Heliotropium arborescens*)

Mignonette (*Reseda odorata*)

Scented geranium (*Pelargonium*)

Stock (*Matthiola*)

Sweet pea (*Lathyrus odoratus*)

CLEVER CONTAINERS

Are your containers housebroken? Flower-packed seasonal pots and new puppies have a lot in common. Both require constant attention and maintenance and can be hard on floors; however, both are also irresistibly appealing for their charm and almost instant impact. Who doesn't love dramatic containers filled to the brim with an abundance of color and texture—or generous sloppy kisses, silky ears, and big brown eyes for that matter?

But high-maintenance container plantings—or puppies—aren't for every household or busy lifestyle. With stylish flair, creativity, and resourcefulness, these projects offer ways to contain your gardening enthusiasm without committing to hours of upkeep.

Plant a table top knot garden for major style points on a miniature scale or pack tons of flavor and delicious eating into a limited space with a back porch herb tower or container orchard. Craft a rustic trough that's a lot lighter than the stone it resembles, or revive an old cedar planter with an artsy copper design and patina finish. And finally, look beyond conventional containers: galvanized gutters and repurposed industrial light fixtures contribute a sophisticated vibe to the modern garden.

Table Top
KNOT GARDEN

Most people don't have the necessary seasonal discipline—or inclination—to maintain a demanding garden feature like a traditional knot garden. Container-bound table top models planted with boxwood cuttings are tiny replicas of the real thing. Pleasingly formal and intricate, these mini-gardens carry the look without all the work and make a much bigger statement than their undersized footprint might suggest.

The creation of formal knot gardens began in Elizabethan England. Rows of dwarf evergreens were planted in intricate geometric patterns based on the design of interior rugs or tapestries and thus were considered "woven" or "knotted." Intended to illustrate the integration of mathematics with the natural world—important concepts to wealthy 16th century landowners with the leisure to ponder such lofty thoughts—these gardens were also a great testament to one's ability to employ the necessary staff for the constant and careful trimming needed to maintain the knot garden's appearance. Botanical boasting as it were.

Shy of staff and short on lofty mathematical thoughts, I simply shrunk the concept down to a more manageable scale. Geometric containers are easy to design with and are a natural match for this formal style of planting. Selecting plants with a dwarf habit or an extremely slow growth rate is critical to the success of your table top knot garden.

If you don't want to take your own boxwood cuttings—a process that adds six to eight months to the project—you can obtain rooted cuttings from your local nursery or order ready-to-plant cuttings online. Table top knot gardens are nearly maintenance free save for an occasional trim with scissors and regular watering. With proper care, your finished planting will endure for years; some of my knot gardens are five years old.

INSTRUCTIONS

➡ **1. Sketch planting plan.** Create a template by tracing the top of your container onto several pieces of scrap paper. Pencil out various designs until you come up with one that pleases you; remember that most formal garden designs are symmetrical, and simple geometric plans read strongly and are easier to maintain.

➡ **2. Prepare container.** Fill your container with dampened potting mix and firmly tap against the surface of your workspace to settle the soil. Using your finger or a pencil, inscribe your final design on the surface of the potting mix. Further define the resulting shallow furrows with small pebbles or dry sand for a clearer preview of your finished plan and an easy-to-follow planting guide.

Boxwood cutting.   *Planting guide.*

➡ **3. Prepare boxwood cuttings.** Gently wash soil away from cuttings and trim roots to an even 1$\frac{1}{2}$ to 2 inches. To encourage future branching, "tip prune" each cutting by snipping the tips of each tiny growing shoot with sharp scissors.

➡ **4. Plant cuttings.** Place each cutting following the lines of your planting guide, spacing plants about 1 inch apart. More mature cuttings which have already begun branching may be planted further apart. Make sure roots are completely covered with soil. Water your finished planted container thoroughly to eliminate air pockets and settle roots into the potting mix.

5. Trim the tiny boxwood plants. Use sharp scissors to nip and neaten the lines of your design. Newly planted rows may initially appear weak and thin, but as young plants establish and flush out with new growth your design will fill in quickly.

Newly planted knot garden.

6. Top-dress finished planting. Completely cover any remaining exposed soil with fine gravel or grit. This final touch helps to set off the design; even very young plantings appear far more finished once "dressed." Topdressing also encourages healthy growth by conserving moisture and maintaining even soil temperatures.

7. Maintain your garden. Boxwood is hardy in zones 6–8. Plants flourish in partial sun to full shade making these little gardens adaptable to just about any exposure. Water regularly during dry weather just as you would any container planting. Clip two or three times a year to maintain shape. Keep plant debris cleared to high-light pattern as well as avoid the accumulation of rotting organic material. Renew topdressing material as needed. Feed with a mild (half-strength) plant food after the first full growing season and every year thereafter.

I am particularly fond of my 16-by-34-inch knot garden planted in a broken down Radio Flyer wagon, a nostalgic remnant from my nursery-owning days.

BOXWOOD ALTERNATIVES

Table top knot gardens can be made with a variety of other woody plants besides boxwood. Note that you probably won't need as many plants since commonly available 4-inch pots are larger than rooted cuttings. You may also find it more difficult to establish nice solid lines right from the start. No worries—just like a "real" hedge or border, plants will branch and knit together in time with routine pinching and trimming. Make sure to trim flowering plants in early spring to shape new growth, and again after blooming to restore outline.

Any of these plants would make a fine substitution for the traditional boxwood, or just mix one into your boxwood-based design for color and textural contrast.

- -

- Dwarf boxleaf variegated euonymus (*Euonymus japonicus* 'Microphyllus Variegatus'). Glossy dark green foliage with tiny leaves splashed with white; evergreen. Deep shade to full sun, zones 6–9.

- Dwarf germander (*Teucrium chamaedrys* 'Nana'). Dark green foliage with late season spikes of purple flowers; evergreen in zones 7 and warmer. Full sun to part shade, zones 5–9.

- Garden thyme (*Thymus vulgaris* and other upright species). Green, gold, and variegated foliage with pale pink flowers in summer. Full sun, zones 4–9.

- Irish yew (*Taxus baccata* 'Stricta'). Slow-growing dark green conifer suitable for shaping on a larger scale; evergreen. Full shade to full sun, zones 4–8.

- Lavender cotton (*Santolina chamaecyparissus*). Silver grey or green foliage with gold button flowers in late summer; evergreen. Full sun, zones 5–10.

Stacking
HERB TOWER

Like an herbal high rise, a tower of stacking galvanized metal containers provides generous pickings for an entire growing season worth of delicious meals. Even if your plot is limited to pots on the patio, fresh herbs and salad greens can yield appetizingly big harvests. The addition of edible flowers, red lettuce, and jeweled strawberries brightens the green color palette of my back porch farmstead.

All containers must have drainage holes. Several of my pots had already rusted through their bases, useless as buckets but perfect for planting. Keep your eyes open at flea markets, tag sales, and recycling stations for similar discards you can put to good use. I've also planted kitchen tins and an imported woven plastic tote for additional layers of flavor, color, and whimsy. The buried bricks and terracotta pots help prevent containers from settling into the soil, keeping their wedding cake–like tiers supported.

Site your tower where it will receive at least six to eight hours of sun a day. Salad greens, bush beans, parsley, and mint will tolerate less light but most edibles need sunny conditions to thrive. Select a quality organic potting mix to get your plants off to a good start—edible crops are only as tasty and nutritious as they are raised to be. Good soil also supports intensive planting and the goal here is to pack as much as we can into a small space.

MATERIALS

3 galvanized metal containers, various sizes; I used a 22-inch washtub, a 15-inch pail, and a 12-inch bucket

INSTRUCTIONS

➡ **1. Prepare containers.** Drill drainage holes every 4 to 6 inches in the bottom of each container. Position bricks or paving stones on your patio or porch surface to support your largest container (in my case, the 22-inch washtub). This slight elevation allows water to drain freely, providing better conditions for the plants and protecting the ground surface. The 15-inch pail sits on a single brick resting

(continued)

- Bricks, paving stones, or old terracotta pots

- 3 cubic feet organic potting soil

- 12 to 15 (4-inch) pots of herbs (See "Suggested Herbs for Container Towers")

- Colorful annuals and seeds (optional)

TOOLS & OTHER SUPPLIES

- Handheld power drill, ¼-inch bit

- Hand trowel

- Scissors or garden snips

on the bottom of the washtub. A stack of terracotta pots raises the 12-inch bucket so that it sits level with the surface of the soil in the middle pail beneath it. This arrangement maximizes the root space herbs need to flourish and generously produce.

➡ **2. Plant containers.** Fill stacked containers with potting mix. Using a hand trowel, transplant herbs, flowers, and salad greens into the potting mix. I planted the bottom tier with summer savory, Thai basil, English thyme, dill, and several variegated flowering nasturtiums. The middle tier is a ring of curly parsley interspersed with ruby orach and sweet marjoram. My largest plant, upright rosemary, which is hardy in my garden and will last for years, is planted in the top bucket along with red basil and more nasturtiums. Keep in mind that perennials need more room as they increase in size each year. Annuals, such as basil, dill, and summer savory, can fit into smaller spaces and spill over the sides of the container. Flowering annuals like nasturtiums and calendulas contribute color and spice to the composition and the salad bowl.

(L) Prepare containers for planting.

(R) The three stacked containers filled with potting soil.

➡ **3. Finish.** Water the finished planting thoroughly to settle soil and roots and eliminate any air pockets.

TRY THIS

Ⓐ *Once the weather turns cold in the fall, replace spent annuals with 4-inch pots of Johnny jump ups (Viola tricolor) for fresh color. In mild winter areas plant salad greens, chard, or kale for a combination that is as pretty as it is delicious.*

Ⓑ *See page 184 for my ornamental terracotta tower variation. I started out stacking pots simply to maximize space, but have since discovered the drama and unexpectedly big impact I get from combining relatively small containers.*

SUGGESTED HERBS FOR CONTAINER TOWERS

Fresh herbs pack more flavor into every square foot of a garden than just about any other edible crop. In addition to a variety of flavors, most herbs yield over an extended harvest period.

- Basil *(Ocimum basilicum)*. Tender green or purple leaves have a spicy perfume and a variety of different flavor profiles, from clove-like to lemon, cinnamon, and spicy Thai. Annual, appreciates warmth and good soil.

- Chervil *(Anthriscus cerefolium)*. Delicate, feathery foliage has a mild anise flavor. Annual, thrives in cool weather and needs protection from hot afternoon sun.

- Chives *(Allium schoenoprasum)*. Fine grass-like blades of young chives emerge early each spring. Mince and sprinkle on food right before serving for a bright oniony snap. Perennial, not fussy about soil.

- Cilantro *(Coriandrum sativum)*. Fragile, flat leafed parsley-like leaves have a strong flavor that is a staple of Mexican and Indian cuisines. Annual, sow successive crops from seed to maintain a steady supply of this quickly growing herb.

- Dill *(Anethum graveolens)*. The feathery fronds and bright yellow flowers have a flavor strongly associated with pickles; also delicious in soups, and fish, potato, or egg dishes. Annual, easy to grow.

- Lemon balm *(Melissa officinalis)*. Slightly fuzzy leaves on sturdy plants have a lemony-mint flavor that brews into a delicious and soothing tea, iced or hot. Perennial, plant in moist shade in its own container to control the vigorous root system.

- Lemon Verbena *(Aloysia triphylla)*. Long, pointed, light green leaves smell and taste strongly of fresh lemons. Woody shrub, plant in full sun and provide winter protection.

- Marjoram *(Origanum majorana)*. Aromatic, small green leaves have a slightly sweet, resinous flavor that pairs well with other Mediterranean herbs. An easy to grow but short-lived perennial, plant in full sun and well-drained soil.

- Mint *(Mentha* species)*. A large family of plants offering a wide range of nuanced flavors from the popular spearmint or peppermint to lemon, pineapple, and ginger. Perennial, plant in moist shade in its own container to control the vigorous root system.

- Parsley *(Petroselinum crispum)*. Ubiquitous but underrated herb with a fresh "green" flavor that is packed with nutrition. Biennial, establish new plants every year to avoid bitterness.

- Pineapple Sage *(Salvia elegans)*. Soft, mint-like foliage with a tropical pineapple fragrance and sweet flavor makes this a favorite for teas and fruit salads. Brilliant red flowers at the end of the growing season attract hummingbirds. Perennial, plant in full sun and well-drained soil.

- Rosemary *(Rosmarinus officinalis)*. Dark green needled branches on a woody shrub lend evergreen structure to the garden. Use sparingly as its strong, coniferous flavor can easily overpower a dish. Drought-tolerant woody shrub, plant in full sun.

- Sage *(Salvia officinalis)*. Soft, velvety leaves with a savory, somewhat camphorous flavor that enhances poultry, egg, and cheese dishes. Woody shrub, grow in full sun and well-drained soil.

- Stevia *(Stevia rebaudiana)*. When harvested, dried and crushed or brewed into a tea, these plain green leaves are ten to fifteen times sweeter than table sugar with a slight licorice aftertaste. Tender perennial, grow as you would basil.

- Summer Savory *(Satureja hortensis)*. Small bushy plant with tiny leaves that taste like a peppery blend of thyme and mint. Annual, grow in full sun and well-drained soil.

- Tarragon *(Artemisia dracunculus)*. Fine, narrow leaves along tender stems have a strong anise flavor. Perennial, plant in full sun to part shade and well-drained soil.

- Thyme *(Thymus vulgaris)*. Tiny, aromatic leaves complement many foods with a peppery flavor and a hint of citrus. Woody perennial, grow in full sun and well-drained soil.

Grow-Anywhere
MINI-ORCHARD

A generously sized agricultural trough planted with a healthful mix of flowering and fruiting plants makes up the orchard aspect of my back porch farmstead. This companion to my stacked herb tower offers height, flowers, fall color, and bold texture in addition to tons of flavor in a space measuring just 4 by 5 feet. Even better, columnar apple trees and rhubarb plants promise future pie!

Purchase agricultural troughs at feed stores, larger pet supply retailers, and increasingly, through resourceful garden centers looking to expand container offerings beyond the expected terracotta and glazed imports. City-centric gardeners may have to daytrip to areas where farm supply warehouses and even neighborhood tag sales turn up troughs in a variety of sizes and conditions. I scored my used trough at a roadside farm sale; having rusted through the bottom in one spot it was no longer functional and was just taking up space in the barnyard.

All containers must have drainage holes, so before you plant your agricultural trough—whether it is shiny brand new or well worn and rusted—you'll need to drill additional holes in the bottom. If your trough already has a large 1- to 2-inch bung hole (used in its agricultural application to quickly drain the container) leave the plug in place or stop up the opening with an old cork, caulk, or even a wadded up cloth. The patch doesn't need to be completely water-fast but you should try to moderate conditions so your container drains evenly.

Make sure to fill your trough generously with potting mix as the level will settle quite a bit after watering. With annual crops it's easy to top up the soil level from year to year; it's another story working around trees and shrubs. Required growing conditions for your container orchard are the same as those for a stacked herb tower. Site your trough where it will receive at least six to eight hours of sun a day and start plants off right with a quality organic potting mix.

MATERIALS

- Agricultural trough; mine is 4 feet long x 2 feet wide x 2 feet deep

- 6 to 8 bricks or small paving stones

- 6 cubic feet organic potting soil

- 2 (5-gallon) columnar apple trees (*Malus*; see "Columnar Apple Trees")

- 2 quart-sized rhubarb plants (*Rheum rhabarbarum*)

- 3 (4-inch) pots chives (*Allium schoenoprasum*)

- 4 (4-inch) pots Santa Barbara daisy (*Erigeron karvinskianus*)

- Colorful annuals and seeds (optional)

TOOLS & OTHER SUPPLIES

- Handheld power drill, 1/4-inch bit

- Tarp

- Short-handled shovel or sturdy trowel

INSTRUCTIONS

➡ **1. Drill holes.** Invert trough and drill a series of drainage holes every 6 to 8 inches in a grid across the bottom of the entire container.

➡ **2. Position trough**. Prop drilled trough on bricks or paving stones so it sits 2 to 3 inches above the surface of the porch or patio. This slight elevation allows water to drain freely, providing better conditions for the plants and protecting the surface beneath the container.

➡ **3. Prepare trough for planting.** Fill trough with potting mix and water thoroughly to help settle the soil; add more soil after watering if necessary to fill the trough. Potting mix will continue to settle but this step greatly reduces that factor.

➡ **4. Plant trough.** Lay out a tarp to help facilitate cleanup and avoid wasting potting mix. Starting with the largest plants (in my case, the 5-gallon columnar apple trees) remove plants from their pots and place them on the tarp. Gently massage root balls with your fingers, loosening roots and removing extra soil. Dig a hole in the potting mix and plant apple trees at the same level they were growing in their containers. Repeat this planting procedure with the rest of your plants working from largest to smallest in size. Small pots of flowering annuals and seeds may be tucked in among the larger plants for instant color and an abundant effect.

➡ **5. Finish.** Water trough to settle plant roots and eliminate remaining air pockets.

TRY THIS

(A) *In partially shaded locations that receive at least six hours of sun throughout the day, plant a pair of 'Sunshine Blue' blueberries* (Vaccinium *'Sunshine Blue'*). *Fill in beneath the attractive fruiting shrubs with shade-tolerant and prolific alpine strawberries* (Fragaria vesca) *whose tiny jewel-like berries pack a flavorful punch. Flower power comes from tuberous begonias that bloom all summer; their succulent petals have a zippy lemonlike flavor and are a delicious and colorful addition to salad, desserts, and even cocktails.*

(B) *In challenging hot conditions in zones 8 and warmer, cultivate a taste of the Mediterranean with a fig tree* (Ficus carica) *underplanted with trailing forms of rosemary* (Rosmarinus officinalis) *and aromatic culinary thyme* (Thymus vulgaris). *Container growing limits the mature size of your fig tree ensuring you can harvest the ripe fruit before birds steal it away.*

COLUMNAR APPLE TREES

Columnar or colonnade fruit trees are relatively new to the market and a real boon to gardeners with limited growing space. Producing a generous harvest of full-size fruit along a central trunk, these naturally dwarf trees reach 8 to 10 feet tall by only 2 feet wide and can be grown in containers or planted just 3 to 4 feet apart in the ground. The trees are not self-pollinating; plant two different varieties that bloom at the same time to assure good fruit set if you or your immediate neighbors are not already growing compatible pollinators. Columnar apple trees produce fruit at an early age and continue to yield for up to twenty years. Hardy in zones 4–9.

- *Malus* 'Golden Sentinel'. Large, sweet, juicy golden fruit similar to a Golden Delicious. This exceptionally disease-resistant variety ripens in mid-September and stores well over the winter.
- *Malus* 'North Pole'. Crisp, juicy, bright red fruit is sweet and delicious. Ripens first among the other columnar varieties, in early September.
- *Malus* 'Scarlet Sentinel'. Large, greenish-yellow fruit blushed with red is sweet and juicy with pure white flesh. This productive and disease-resistant variety ripens in late September.

Rustic
FEATHERWEIGHT TROUGH

Lend instant rustic antiquity and craggy character to your garden with a collection of stonelike containers that are easily crafted from hardware store materials. These durable, frost-proof planters are commonly referred to as hypertufa, a reference to "tufa," the naturally occurring volcanic stone which they replicate. Such porous surfaces continue to improve with age, culturing a weathered moss- or lichen-encrusted patina depending on environmental conditions.

The process is satisfyingly similar to messing around with mud pies. The ingredients are basic and can be found at any hardware store or home warehouse. Coco coir, a natural by-product of the coconut industry, may be substituted for the more environmentally questionable peat moss. Portland cement comes in standard 47-pound bags; economical, but a beast to carry and way more than you'll need for this recipe. Store leftover cement in a sealed bag or lidded container, keeping it dry until your next hypertufa session. Better yet, scale up the recipe and invite friends over for an afternoon of playing in the mud.

Cement colorants may be added to dry ingredients to alter the natural grey finish of Portland cement. You'll find these powdered pigments (typically used as a coloring agent for grout) with tiling supplies at hardware stores and home centers. Any sort of plastic container is suitable for a mold but I especially like rectangular shapes. My finished trough measures 12 by 16 inches and has a blocky sturdiness, appearing convincingly weighty without the heft of real stone.

Rubber gloves, a dust mask, and "play clothes" offer protection from irritating dust and caustic lime in the Portland cement. Just like mud creations, this project is best undertaken outdoors. Note that at least five weeks are required for the trough to fully cure and weather before you can plant it.

MATERIALS

- 1 bale (3 cubic feet) peat moss or coco coir

- 1 bag (¹/₂ cubic foot) coarse builder's sand

- 1 bag (47 pound) Portland cement

- Cement colorant (optional)

- 4 to 6 (4-inch) pots of mixed succulents

- Well-drained potting mix

- Fine gravel or granite grit (optional)

TOOLS & OTHER SUPPLIES

- Rubber gloves

- Dust mask

- Plastic sheeting or tarp

- Small plastic bucket or scoop

- Wheelbarrow or large plastic tub

- Hand trowel

- Watering can

- 2 kitchen-sized plastic garbage bags

- 1 (12 x 16-inch) plastic storage drawer for mold

- Clothespins

- Stiff brush, stick, or chisel

1. Protect work area. Cover an outdoor work surface like a picnic table or potting bench with plastic sheeting or a tarp.

2. Mix dry ingredients. Using a small plastic bucket or scoop as a measuring unit, combine 3 parts peat moss, 3 parts sand, and 2 parts Portland cement in a wheelbarrow or large plastic tub. Sift and crumble peat moss or coco coir to remove lumps and clods, reducing the material to a uniform fine consistency. Stir dry ingredients with a hand trowel until you have a well-mixed blend. If you are using cement colorant, add the powdered pigment at this stage and mix well. Keep in mind that a little pigment goes a long way and a mere cast of color appears more natural than a lurid finished hue.

3. Add water. Slowly add water to the dry ingredients, a cup at a time, to form a pliable mixture with the consistency of cottage cheese. You should be able to form a handful of the mixture into a firm ball and have it hold its shape. Let the mixture rest for five minutes to allow the peat or coir to fully absorb the moisture; add more water if necessary to reach the proper consistency.

Materials measured out for mixing.

Finished form in mold.

⇒ **4. Line mold with plastic.** While the mix is resting, cut a garbage bag open along the sides so you have a large sheet of plastic. Line storage drawer mold with plastic, making sure the entire inside area is covered. Hold plastic in place with clothespins.

⇒ **5. Form base.**
Scoop a handful of the wet mix into your lined mold. Using your knuckles, tamp and pack the base solidly as if forming a graham cracker crumb crust in a tart pan. The finished base should be at least 1½ to 2 inches deep depending on the finished size of your trough; larger containers should have a more substantial base. Insert a dowel or poke your finger into the base in several places to create drainage holes.

⇒ **6. Form sides.** With the base completed, begin to pack the mixture up the sides of your mold, tamping firmly to form walls that are a ½-inch thinner than the base.

⇒ **7. Initial cure.** Place your completed trough, still in its mold, into the other garbage bag and set aside to cure for 24 to 48 hours out of direct sunlight. A longer curing time results in a firmer set although you want the material soft enough to clean up and apply finishing touches.

(continued)

8. Unmold trough. Remove your trough by turning the mold upside down and gently tapping its bottom to release the form. Handle with care—the planter has not yet cured to its full strength.

9. Apply finishing touches. Your newly unmolded planter will retain a smooth surface broken only by a replica of the wrinkles in the plastic. Using a stiff brush, gently texture and rough up the outside for a more suitably rustic finish; deeper gouges made with a stick, file, or screwdriver simulate the markings of hand-carved stone.

10. Final cure. Place your trough back into the garbage bag and set aside for two weeks to complete curing. Tuck the plastic-wrapped trough under a potting bench, beneath the back stairs, or anywhere in the garden out of direct sunlight. The slower this curing period the stronger your finished container will be. In hot, dry climates, keep humidity high by unwrapping the trough and sprinkling with water every few days. Always re-wrap with plastic and return your piece to a cool, shaded location to finish curing.

11. Leach trough. After curing, unwrap and set your finished trough outdoors to thoroughly dry and weather for at least another three weeks. Rain—or watering with a hose in the absence of rain—will neutralize the alkaline nature of the raw cement in your planter. Be careful to not let the container drain into your garden where leaching might damage plantings; a bed of gravel or an out-of-the-way workspace is ideal.

12. Plant trough. Unpot a colorful assortment of sedums and succulents and plant in well-drained potting or cactus mix. Top-dress plantings with fine gravel or granite grit for a rugged but finished look.

TRY THIS

A — *Create an alpine composition of dwarf conifers and tiny, resilient groundcovers accented with a chunk of real stone for a little mountain vignette.*

B — *Troughs intended for shady locations may be filled with velvety mosses and small ferns for a pocket woodland planting.*

LARGER MOLDS AND TOUGHER TROUGHS

Oversized, sink-like troughs have a certain gravitas and dignity. However, with size comes weight and the container mix must be reinforced to support its larger bulk. Fibermesh, a concrete reinforcing product sold by lumberyards and concrete suppliers, is the key to supporting larger troughs. These instructions are for a finished trough measuring roughly 20 x 15 inches.

MATERIALS

- *All the materials in the main recipe (except for the mold)*
- *1 sheet rigid foam insulation, 24 x 96 inches*
- *Utility knife*
- *8 to 10 bamboo kitchen skewers*
- *Duct tape*
- *1 bag Fibermesh*
- *Propane torch or fireplace lighter (optional)*

INSTRUCTIONS

1. Create mold. Using a sharp utility blade, cut foam insulation sheet into two 21 x 6-inch rectangles and two 15 x 6-inch rectangles to form the outer sides of the mold. Attach these four pieces into a rectangular bottomless box by pinning the corners together with short lengths of bamboo kitchen skewers. Secure seams, inside and out, with duct tape. Repeat the process with two 15 x 3-inch rectangles and two 10 x 3-inch rectangles to form a smaller box. Placed inside the first box, this smaller box will shape the cavity of your finished piece forming a 3-inch base and 2 $1/2$-inch walls.

2. Position mold. Place the larger box on a level work surface where the trough can remain undisturbed for two to three days. Line the mold with plastic.

3. Mix ingredients. Strengthen the basic recipe by adding $1/2$ cup of Fibermesh to every gallon of dry mix in step 2 of "Rustic Featherweight Trough." Add water as outlined in step 3. With larger molds it is especially important to avoid adding too much water to the mix because that will weaken the finished container.

4. Fill mold. Firmly pack wet mixture into the larger box to form a base 3-inches thick. Create drainage holes by inserting a dowel or poking your finger into the base in several places. Center the smaller box on top of the packed base and carefully fill the space between the inner and outer walls with more wet mixture; tamp and pack as you build to eliminate air pockets.

5. Cure and unmold trough. Cover the finished trough with plastic and set aside to cure for two to three days. Unmold trough by removing tape and disassembling the larger, outer box. Remove the inner form. Brush, gouge, and carve until the trough is roughed up to your liking.

6. Finish curing trough. Wrap the trough in plastic and cure out of direct sunlight for at least two weeks, misting as necessary to maintain moisture. Remember, the slower the cure the stronger the finished trough. Allow an additional two weeks of weathering or watering for the larger trough to neutralize.

7. Remove Fibermesh remnants. Once the trough has completely cured and dried, the protruding "hairs" of Fibermesh may be burned off with a propane torch or fireplace lighter. Keep the flame moving quickly so as not to overheat any remaining damp pockets and risk exploding your work.

COPPER & CEDAR PLANTER

This striking copper-clad planter box carries the show with a supporting cast of textural, blond ornamental grasses and drought-resistant perennials that shimmer in the slightest breeze. The simple angular lines of the box contrast with the loose planting style for a sophisticated but casual effect and a beach vibe so fresh you can almost smell the salt air. Its new copper surface adds panache while the patina finish complements the aged cedar for a look that's more valued garden antique than cast-off garden giveaway. See "Instant Patina" for an easy homemade solution that produces an authentic weathered look.

I used an old cedar planter that was showing its age—and not in a good way. If you don't already have a planter ripe for a makeover, wooden boxes are stock items at most garden centers. Soft, fine gauge copper can be cut with a pair of old scissors, just be careful around the resulting sharp edges. It's available from a number of sources: hardware stores and lumber yards sell rolls of copper flashing as termite barrier, craft stores stock sheet copper and adhesive copper tape for art projects, while nurseries and garden centers sell rolls of copper barrier as an organic slug ad snail control.

MATERIALS

- Wooden planter box; mine is 12 inches tall x 48 inches wide x 18 inches deep

- 1 roll copper flashing, 8 inches wide x 20 feet long

- Thumbtacks

INSTRUCTIONS

▶ **1. Measure coverage.** Calculate the size and number of copper strips you will need to cut by figuring out the square footage of the surface of your planter. The side of my planter measures 12 x 48 inches, which comes to 4 square feet; (height × width = x ÷ 12 inches = square footage). Because the finished copper surface is woven solid, I need double that amount, or roughly 8 square feet to cover the entire surface. My pattern is not uniform but composed of 1-, 2-, and 3-inch wide strips arranged randomly into an irregular finished weave.

(continued)

MATERIALS (CONT.)

- Upholstery tacks, brads, or small nails

- 3 cubic feet potting soil

- 3 (1-gallon) pots Mexican feather grass (*Nassella tenuissima*)

- 2 (1-gallon) pots Black-eyed Susan (*Rudbeckia subtomentosa* 'Henry Eilers')

- 1 (2-gallon) pot pheasant grass (*Anemanthele lessoniana*)

TOOLS & OTHER SUPPLIES

- Measuring stick

- Ballpoint pen

- Old scissors

- Rubber mallet

- Spray bottle

- Plastic sheeting or garbage bag

2. Cut horizontal copper strips. Lay copper flashing out on a level work surface; measure and cut four 48-inch lengths. Using the measuring stick and a ballpoint pen, horizontally divide two 8-inch wide flashing strips each into one 3-inch; two 2-inch; and one 1-inch strip. With old scissors, carefully cut along the incised pen lines in long, even slices for a smooth, non-ragged edge.

3. Pin horizontal strips in place. Position flashing strips, nestling one up against the other for complete coverage working from the top of the planter down, using thumbtacks to pin strips in position at both ends and the middle of each length. My strip placement pattern—3-inch, 2-inch, 1-inch, 1-inch, 2-inch, 3-inch—produces strong edges top and bottom with a ribbon of more intricate detail running through the center. Note that you will end up with two extra 2-inch wide strips which you'll use in the course of weaving.

4. Cut remaining copper strips. As in step 2, using the measuring stick and a ballpoint pen, horizontally divide the two remaining 8-inch wide flashing strips each into one 3-inch; three 1-inch; and one 2-inch strip. Cut finished strips to 12-inch lengths or long enough to span the height of your planter box.

5. Weave vertical strips through foundation of horizontal strips. Utilize a simple alternating over and under pattern, staggering different widths for contrast and detail. Tack strips into place to hold their position and check your work often to maintain straight lines and a snug weave.

6. Fix woven strips permanently into place. Use a rubber mallet to pound upholstery tacks, brads, or small nails into place at each side and along the top and bottom of the planter. Supplementary fastening points across the face of the planter

Pounding the woven copper pattern into place.

help hold the weaving in place and contribute an additional layer of surface decor.

➡ **7. Finish.** Apply patina (see "Instant Patina") before filling planter with potting mix and plants.

TRY THIS

- -

(A) *Alter your pattern by leaving open space within your weave so the surface of the wooden planter shows through.*

(B) *Forgo weaving altogether: cut simple copper shapes from copper flashing and attach to planters, fences, or any other wooden surface in the garden.*

Generously applied, even humble materials can form highly decorative and expressive surface treatments, like this nail-head totem.

INSTANT PATINA

Over time and with exposure to weather, copper naturally develops a beautiful blue-green patina or verdigris finish. This effect is especially pronounced in coastal areas where seawater and salty breezes accelerate the natural oxidation process. But if your garden lacks a maritime influence, or you just want to speed things along, you can easily create an almost-instant weathered patina to copper, brass, and bronze surfaces.

Take caution when working with ammonia, a noxious and potentially dangerous chemical. Minimize your exposure to toxic fumes by working outdoors in a well-ventilated area. Dilute leftover ammonia with water and pour down the drain—do not dispose of it in septic systems.

MATERIALS

- *Grease-cutting household cleaner*
- *4 tablespoons table salt*
- *5 ounces cider or distilled white vinegar*
- *1 cup ammonia*

TOOLS AND OTHER SUPPLIES

- *Soft cloth or rag*
- *Plastic spray bottle*
- *Wide-mouth bowl*
- *Plastic sheeting or garbage bag*

INSTRUCTIONS

1. Prepare copper surface. Thoroughly wipe down copper surface with a soft cloth and grease-cutting household cleaner to remove oils and dirt which resist the applied finish. Avoid touching the cleaned surface as even the oils on your fingers will leave marks in the finish.

2. Apply solution.
In a plastic spray bottle, dissolve 4 tablespoons of table salt in 5 ounces of cider or distilled white vinegar. Lightly spritz copper with the vinegar and salt solution to initiate the oxidation process. For quicker results, place a wide-mouthed bowl of household ammonia next to the sprayed surface of your copper planter. Drape the planter with plastic sheeting or a garbage bag to enclose the bowl and trap the ammonia fumes.

Fuming tent for an almost-instant patina.

3. Let patina develop. A brilliant verdigris finish will begin forming as the salt, vinegar, and ammonia interact with the copper. Do not disturb the fuming tent for at least two hours before checking on the progress of the developing finish. The process is not exact and may take up to twice as long to achieve the strength of color desired.

4. Finish. Remove the plastic bag being careful to avoid breathing the escaping nasty fumes. Allow the now "weathered" surface of your planter to fully dry.

A BIRD-FREE BIRDBATH

This broken down, once-discarded concrete birdbath now has a
new lease on life and pride of place in my garden. In the past I've planted
it with the more expected mix of sedums and succulents, but this year
I wanted something lush, animated, and rich. Spilling from the canted lip
of the basin: deep blue annual lobelia (*Lobelia erinus*), foaming silver
groundcovers (*Dichondra argentea* 'Silver Falls', *Sutera cordata*, and *Lotus
berthelotii*), and Magellan wheatgrass (*Elymus magellanicus*). Planted
in shallow potting soil amended with water-holding polymers it forms a
botanical caricature of flowing water; my very own plant pun.

Sleek
SUCCULENT GUTTER

This shiny, sleek planter—actually a modified length of pedestrian galvanized gutter—takes up little room on a tiny balcony but contributes flash and a lively mix of color and texture from succulent plants as tough as the metal is durable. The resulting contemporary composition is stylish and hip— a far cry from planting an old boot.

Succulents are perfect for planting in shallow containers on hot decks that bake in the afternoon sun; in locations beyond the reach of the hose that still cry out for some vegetative wonder; or in non-traditional planters which you'd never be able to keep watered under average summer conditions. See "Sassy Succulents" (page 153) for a more detailed look at these garden survivors.

Galvanized gutters come in 10-foot lengths at most lumber yards and hardware stores so you'll probably need to cut your gutter into shorter lengths before transporting it home. It's my experience that the good people at these establishments will not make metal cuts, therefore you'll need to bring your own tin snips and protective gloves when purchasing your material—it's not often we get to start a project while still on the sales floor. This project is completed in two phases: permit the construction adhesive to thoroughly set up and dry overnight before finishing, installing, and planting your gutter.

MATERIALS

- Galvanized gutter; I cut mine to 45 inches long
- 2 gutter end caps (1 left, 1 right)
- Potting soil
- Pumice
- 16 (4-inch) pots mixed succulents

INSTRUCTIONS

➡ **1. Measure selected space.** To prevent sagging, limit finished length of your gutter planter to 48 inches or shorter.

➡ **2. Cut gutter to size.** Lay your gutter atop a flat work surface. Measure off 45 inches (or whatever fits your space) and use Sharpie pen to mark this point along the inside back, the center well, and the inside front edge of the gutter. Connect these dots with the Sharpie

(continued)

to create a cutting guide. Snip along the cutting guide starting at the front edge of the gutter. Turning corners is awkward but try not to twist or distort the metal as you cut. It is easier to work toward the center and then start again from the backside and snip to meet your first cut. Trim cut ends neatly, removing any ragged edges or loose snags.

→ **3. Add end caps.** Fit right gutter end cap onto the right end of the gutter; use pliers to straighten cut edges for a good clean fit and tap securely into place with the rubber mallet. Pinch edges of end cap securely over edges of the gutter with pliers. Following package instructions, apply heavy-duty construction adhesive along the inside seam where the end cap and the gutter meet. Repeat this procedure to fit the left end cap in place. Allow glue to set up overnight.

Tap end caps securely into place with a rubber mallet.

→ **4. Prepare and mount gutter.** Drill holes every 4 inches along the bottom of your gutter to provide drainage for your container planting. Drill five mounting holes at the top of the gutter along the back; one at each end and three more every 12 inches. Holding the gutter in position, mark mounting points on the deck railing with a pencil; drill pilot holes. Securely fasten the gutter to the railing with wood screws.

➡ **5. Plant gutter.** Mix 2 parts potting soil and 1 part pumice together in your bucket. Fill your mounted gutter-turned-container with the resulting lightweight, well-drained planting mix. Remove plants from their pots, loosen their root balls, and plant into gutter. Fill gaps in your arrangement with small divisions of groundcover sedums and hens 'n chicks to create a solid tapestry of mixed shapes, colors, and textures. Water your finished planting to settle roots and soil.

Planting detail, left to right: Sedum reflexum *'Blue Spruce'*, Graptopetalum, Sedum spurium, *and* Kalanchoe luciae.

TRY THIS

A *Turn a blank fence into a living wall by mounting several staggered tiers of succulent-planted gutter containers.*

B *For a vertical vegetable garden, fill sassy gutters with rich organic potting mix and then plant leafy edibles or shallow root vegetables like radishes and round baby carrots. Place a lightweight soaker hose along the length of the gutter to help keep these thirstier plants hydrated.*

A plucky pair of planted toasters proves anything and everything is fair game for potting. Garden of Johanna and Richard Marquis.

OUTDOOR TERRARIUM

Create a unique garden feature by transforming an industrial light fixture into an outdoor terrarium—a completely contained and balanced, self-sufficient world of plants and humidity.

With its chic, oversized, ridged base, the salvaged light fixture I'd been using as a quirky side table on our deck was a surefire conversation piece, but its empty interior begged filling. Relocated to a sheltered nook in our side yard and planted with shade-tolerant perennials—lime green club moss, delicate ferns, and peachy-colored coral bells accented by annual impatiens in tropical hues—my funky table-turned-terrarium is a real showstopper that thrives on benign neglect.

Don't worry if you can't find a similar light fixture—a variety of other transparent glass containers can be converted into stunning outdoor terrariums. An old aquarium, a lidded jar, a large vase covered with a glass plate, or a garden cloche placed atop a glazed container all impart their individual style to the finished composition: modern, vintage, sleek, or ornate.

Outdoor terrariums must be sited in dappled to full shade. When positioning large containers not easily moved once planted, factor in changing sun patterns throughout the summer; even a short period of direct sun through the glass will cook plants inside. The area beneath the spreading branches of a mature conifer offers ideal conditions for an outdoor terrarium, transforming empty dry shade into a lush garden focal point.

Plant your terrarium like you would any other container, with the addition of a bottom layer of pebbles (for drainage) and activated charcoal (to keep the soil sweet and prevent stagnation). You'll find charcoal at garden centers or aquarium supply stores. Plants should take up no more than about one-third of the interior volume of your terrarium leaving plenty of room for growth.

MATERIALS

- Closed or lidded glass container; my light fixture is 27 inches in diameter x 18 inches deep

- Metal hardware cloth, 6 x 6-inch piece

- Weed barrier fabric, 6 x 6-inch piece

- 1 quart ($^1/_4$-inch) washed gravel

- Activated charcoal

- 1 cubic foot soilless potting mix

- 1 (1-gallon) nursery pot 'Caramel' coral bells (*Heuchera villosa* 'Caramel')

- 2 (4-inch) pots exotic impatiens (*Impatiens hybrida*)

- 3 (4-inch) pots golden spikemoss (*Selaginella kraussiana* 'Aurea')

- 3 (4-inch) pots Himalayan maidenhair fern (*Adiantum venustum*)

TOOLS & OTHER SUPPLIES

- Trowel

- Watering can

1. Site terrarium. Position container in garden if it will be too heavy to move after planting. If your container has an open base (mine has a 4-inch hole that used to accommodate wiring), cover it with a scrap of metal hardware cloth topped by a piece of weed barrier fabric. This will prevent pests and critters from getting into the terrarium.

2. Add bottom layer. Distribute a 1-inch layer of gravel mixed with a generous handful of activated charcoal.

Light fixture base.

3. Plant terrarium. Add moistened potting soil to 8 inches, or deep enough to accommodate your largest root ball. Arrange plants in potting mix, loosening roots so they quickly establish into the new environment. Top up planting with additional potting mix and water thoroughly to settle roots and soil and eliminate any air pockets.

Finished planting.

▶ **4. Tidy up.** Wash down interior glass walls to remove any soil or debris. Place glass lid over container and monitor closely for a day or so to make certain your light and shade calculations are accurate. You may need to prop up the glass lid on newly established plantings to vent excess condensation until an interior balance of plant growth, light, and moisture is attained.

TRY THIS

Plant a woodland-themed outdoor terrarium with a foundation of lacy ferns and delicate groundcovers like baby tears (Soleirolia soleirolii) *and strawberry begonia* (Saxifraga stolonifera). *Further emulate the forest floor by accessorizing your composition with twigs, sheet moss, and a mulch of shredded bark.*

PLANTS IN MY GLOWING OUTDOOR TERRARIUM

The key to my successful terrarium is that all of the plants thrive under the same conditions: partial to full shade and evenly moist, well-drained soil. Keep this concept in mind when adapting plant selections to your particular container, climate, and taste.

- 'Caramel' coral bells *(Heuchera villosa* 'Caramel'*)*. Ruffled velvety leaves are a yummy color of burnt sugar and peaches with a darker raspberry reverse. An evergreen perennial growing to 24 inches tall; clip any leaves touching the glass top of your outdoor terrarium by the end of the growing season. Zones 4–9.

- Exotic impatiens *(Impatiens hybrida)*. An old fashioned favorite, now available in the warm colors of a tropical sunset. Low-mounding plants produce masses of delicate, orchid-like flowers all summer long. Annual.

- Golden spikemoss *(Selaginella kraussiana* 'Aurea'*)*. The soft ferny texture and glowing golden yellow foliage of this low groundcover lights up the shade. Not a true moss and more closely related to ferns. Zones 7–9.

- Himalayan maidenhair fern *(Adiantum venustum)*. A diminutive fern growing just 6 inches tall and spreading slowly. Elegant lacy fronds along black stems present a delicate appearance belying a tough constitution. Zones 5–8.

From hardy perennials and groundcovers to exotic and tender plants more commonly grown as houseplants, undemanding succulents are the stuff of container gardening dreams. Shallow-rooted succulents store water in their fleshy stems and leaves, enabling them to withstand long periods of drought and actually flourish under challenging conditions and occasional neglect. Almost without exception these plants require full sun to part shade and well-drained soil which is allowed to dry between waterings. Overwinter plants indoors under lights or on a sunny windowsill where not hardy.

Sassy Succulents

ALOES

(Aloe)

Architectural stemless clumps of whorled, fleshy, pointed leaves, many with spiny margins. Foliage color varies from grey to bright green; some varieties have leaves that are striped, mottled with cream, or blushed with bronze. Tubular flowers in yellow, pink, or red appear in summer.

ZONES 9–11.

CRASSULAS

(Crassula)

Sculptural form and fleshy leaves, sometimes arranged with geometric precision, lend quirky character and substance to succulent plantings. This large family of plants includes mat-forming groundcovers, mounding clumps, and upright treelike forms such as the commonly grown jade plant.

ZONES 8–9.

ECHEVERIAS

(Echeveria)

Beautiful, broad rosettes of succulent leaves come in a variety of colors from straight green to luminous lavender, metallic rose, and glowing silver; many have contrasting colored margins. Varieties with ruffled, crimped, and wavy foliage lend an undersea-like effect. Tall spires of nodding, bell-shaped, pink, coral, or red flowers bloom in winter.

ZONES 9–11.

HENS 'N CHICKS

(Sempervivum)

These familiar rock garden denizens have undergone a horticultural industry makeover in recent years shedding their drab green garb and emerging in chic new colors that include wine red, sea foam teal, silver grey, and rosy salmon. Tightly packed evergreen rosettes spread by offsets, requiring only a shallow pocket of soil.

ZONES 3–11.

SEDUMS

(Sedum)

This large family of plants includes hardy groundcovers, resilient perennials, and tender exotics. Foliage type varies dramatically from glossy, jelly bean–like leaves or soft, narrow foliage on lax stems, to upright, fleshy stalks with broad succulent leaves. Small, star-shaped flowers appear on wiry stems above groundcovers or in tight rounded clusters on upright plants.

HARDINESS VARIES BY SPECIES.

FINISHING TOUCHES

Like the unexpected sprinkling of coarse sea salt on an artisanal chocolate caramel, the right finishing touch in the garden is a stroke of genius, taking a good thing over the top into brilliance. Gilding the lily you say? I hope so.

A collection of plants, however choice and brilliantly well-tended, doesn't become a real garden until it takes on the character and personality of the gardener behind it. The best gardens—those we fall into for hours, appearing new with every visit—are ones in which the owners are telling us something. These landscapes read like a good story, revealing layers of detail and an individual signature that distinguishes their space from every other yard on the block. Masterful storytellers bring characters and scenes to life with detail and nuance; likewise, finishing touches, ornaments, and offbeat art add subtle—or sometimes not-so-subtle—savor to a garden's unique tale.

I hope the heart-on-your-sleeve projects in this chapter inspire you to spin some garden stories of your own. Whimsical but songbird-approved birdbaths provide winged entertainment along with their pastel glimmer. Three very different outdoor lighting projects cast their magical glow on the landscape after sundown whether romancing an intimate nook, illuminating the gentle curve of a pathway, or shedding a delightful firefly sparkle into dark corners and secret gardens. And don't forget to have some serious fun with garden art—even wrangling stubborn garden hoses and labeling plants can be entertaining with the right accessories.

Glimmering
GLASS BIRDBATHS

A successful birdbath is not the most elaborate, the wittiest, or even the prettiest: it's the one that gets used. Birds animate the garden with movement and song and I find watching their comic antics endlessly appealing. The fact that they devour aphids, caterpillars, and other pests is a wonderful added bonus. While it may be true that most birds would actually prefer a shallow pool or mud puddle, a sparkling water basin has its own appeal and is a well-loved, traditional garden ornament.

In this project, glass ceiling lamps are transformed into charmingly decorative and functional birdbaths pleasing to gardener and bird alike. Vintage fixtures can be found in antique stores and salvage yards but brand new lamp fittings work just as well. Glass is easy to keep clean, a vital component of maintaining a healthy birdbath. Hung from lightweight chain and adorned with sparkling chandelier crystals or suspended by simple sturdy display hooks, the shimmering basins gently sway in the branches of a sheltering tree or shrub. Given the inherently fragile nature of glass, remove your hanging birdbath in windy weather and over the winter.

MATERIALS

For the pink model:

- Glass lamp fixture; mine is 10 inches in diameter x 3 inches deep, with 3 mounting holes

- 14 gauge galvanized wire

- 3 (24-inch-long) strong wire double-ended hooks

- Hanging hook (must be able to fit over branch)

- Tumbled white glass

INSTRUCTIONS

➡ **1. Prepare ceiling lamp fixture**. *For the pink model:* cut three 6-inch lengths of 14 gauge wire and wind each one around the wooden dowel forming tight corkscrews about an inch long. Working carefully, screw wire corkscrews into each hole on the lamp bowl. Each corkscrew should fit tightly, protruding about $1/2$ inch into the interior of the bowl. Trim extra wire. A dab of silicone caulk fills the remaining gap around the corkscrews, allowing the pink birdbath to be filled beyond the depth of the holes, but keep wires on the inside of the bowl free to receive hooks. Allow silicone to dry completely before proceeding with the following steps.

(continued)

MATERIALS (CONT.)

For the frosted model:

- Glass lamp fixture; mine is 12 inches in diameter x 4 inches deep, with 1 hole at bottom center

- 2 (6-foot) lengths light-weight black chain

- Small black hook

- Hanging hook (must be able to fit over branch)

- Tumbled glass, mixed greens and blue

- Chandelier crystals

TOOLS & OTHER SUPPLIES

- Wire cutters

- Short wooden dowel, ½-inch diameter

- Needle-nose pliers

- Silicone caulk

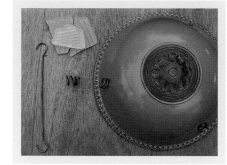 

Materials for pink model.   *Materials for frosted model.*

For the frosted model: fill the hole at the bottom of the lamp fixture with silicone caulk so it holds water. Allow silicone to dry completely before proceeding with the following steps.

➡ **2. Hang birdbath.** Position hanging hooks where you want your finished piece to hang; make sure to choose sturdy branches that will support the weight of the filled birdbath.

For the pink model: attach a 24-inch doubled-ended hook to each mounted wire corkscrew on the inside of the glass bowl. Gather the opposite ends of the long hooks together and suspend as a unit from hanging hook.

Hanging detail.

For the frosted model: double two 6-foot lengths of black chain into two 3-foot loops and four loose ends. Thread the loose ends of the black chain onto the small black hook. Suspend black hook and the looping chains from the hanging hook. Carefully nestle the frosted glass bowl into an "X" formed by crisscrossing the hanging looped chains; adjust each of the four chains so they are positioned evenly around the edge and the fixture hangs level.

▶ **3. Finishing touches.** Add tumbled glass to birdbath basins to provide a secure perch 1¹/₂ to 2 inches below the surface of the water.

For the frosted model: hook chandelier crystals to black chain so they hang freely.

TRY THIS

A *Less girly, more grunge. Drill four evenly spaced holes around the edge of a galvanized garbage can lid. Attach chain and suspend from a sturdy branch.*

B *Some bird species actually prefer low baths. Set an altered lamp bowl atop a columnar terracotta pot or chimney flue to create a more grounded version.*

C *No trees? Hang your birdbath from an antique birdcage stand nestled among shrubs in a secure corner of the garden.*

BIRDBATH BASICS

To be sure, flashing feathers, antic flight, and birdsong enliven the garden. Before you encourage birds to linger in your garden, familiarize yourself with some guidelines to protect their health and well being.

- Until their feathers dry, birds can't fly and remain vulnerable to neighborhood cats and larger birds. Site your birdbath near the shelter of trees or a shrub so they have a safe place to perch and preen following their bath.

- Keep birdbath water fresh and the basin clean. A position in partial shade keeps the water cool, controlling the growth of algae and bacteria which could sicken birds. Routinely scrub your birdbath and rinse with a mild bleach solution (9:1 water to bleach) to disinfect. Allow the birdbath to thoroughly dry before refilling.

- Birds are unable to judge water depth. A relatively shallow, sloping basin provides secure footing for birds wading into the water. If your birdbath does not have sloping sides, create a non-slippery perch by filling the basin with sand, gravel, or tumbled glass. Or place a twig across the top of the birdbath.

- A still birdbath—or any standing water like that which accumulates in plant saucers, buckets, and faultily draining gutters—offers ideal breeding conditions for mosquitoes. At best, buzzing mosquitoes are an unwelcome and annoying garden pest; at worst, they are a vector for the debilitating West Nile virus. To reduce your risk of exposure to this disease, and for a more pleasant garden-sitting experience, empty and refresh birdbaths every day during warm summer months when mosquitoes are present.

Tree-Hung
VINTAGE CHANDELIER

Outdoor mood lighting is all about creating ambiance and a unique setting outside the glare of everyday life. The congeniality of a porch light, the blaze of a backyard bonfire, or strings of carnival lights foster spirited festivities. The glow of this candlelit chandelier suspended from the limbs of a venerable Japanese maple casts a sense of quiet intimacy and dare I say it—romance.

The kinks and curves of old fashioned hairpin wire garden edging add flair to what is simply a basic cylinder. New wire edging is available at most garden centers and hardware stores but I'm always scouting garage sales and flea markets for lengths of heavier gauge, vintage goods which often have more detail. While you're at the hardware store, pick up these clear glass jelly jar–style porch light covers whose ridged sides beautifully refract candlelight. Adorn your finished chandelier with faceted glass crystals and beads which will catch and reflect the flickering flames of the votive candles. Vintage crystals and drops may be salvaged or purchased at antique stores, but brand-new craft store versions are perfectly acceptable too.

MATERIALS

- Heavy-duty, wire hairpin edging, 48 x 22 inches
- 16 and 20 gauge galvanized wire
- 3 jelly jar–style glass porch light covers
- 10 to 12 cut-glass crystals
- 3 votive candles

INSTRUCTIONS

➡ **1. Form cylinder.** Shape wire edging into a 16-inch cylinder, joining cut ends and wrapping securely with 16 gauge wire. Turn cylinder upside down so the top curves now form the scalloped bottom of the chandelier. Bend loose wire spokes toward the center.

(continued)

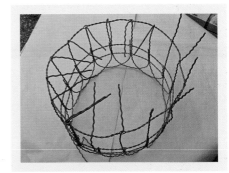

Shaping cylinder.

2. Construct hanging framework. Cut two 18-inch lengths of 16 gauge wire and wrap them around outer rim of the wire cylinder crisscrossing them at right angles at the center of the cylinder; trim loose ends. Secure the midpoint (where the wires cross) by wrapping it with a short length of 16 gauge wire. Wind a roughly 48-inch length of 20 gauge wire twice around the top of the chandelier about 4 inches in from the outside edge, weaving the spokes and cross-braces together. Use pliers to crimp and cinch into a tight circle which will support the individual lanterns.

Top detail.

3. Wire jelly jar lanterns. Cut a 24-inch length of 16 gauge wire for each hanging lantern. Fold wire in half and use pliers to crimp tightly just beneath the fold. Wrap the folded end around a pencil or the handle of a wooden spoon forming a hook. With the base of the hook held firmly with pliers, separate the two wires and twist them tightly together twice; 5 inches below this twist, form a right angled bend with pliers in each wire. Place bends on opposite sides of glass light cover, fitting wires into the notch just below the top rim. Working in reverse directions, wrap wires around the glass until they meet the opposite bend; trim extra wire leaving just enough length to form small hooks on the cut ends. Attach hooks to adjacent bends creating a cuff to hold the jar securely.

Hanging lanterns.

4. Decorate chandelier. Attach crystals with thin wire around the lower scalloped edge of the cylinder.

5. Final assembly. Position lanterns by hooking them to the top interlaced wires of the frame balancing the weight evenly so your finished chandelier hangs level. Place votive candles in lanterns and light them. Then suspend your chandelier from the branch of a tree or other garden hook.

TRY THIS

A *Spread the light and love by hanging individual lanterns from branches and hooks scattered around the garden.*

B *Create a smaller, almost instant version of a garden chandelier by suspending votives crafted from glass yogurt containers or baby food jars from an upside down, vintage wire egg basket.*

C *Allow your candlelit chandelier to play an equally romantic role by day. Repurpose glass lanterns as vases to hold casual arrangements of cut blossoms and tendrils of flowering vines for a charming hanging bouquet.*

Flowering sweet pea and clematis vines entwined with the glossy foliage of star jasmine are a dreamy tangle of color and fragrance.

Tap-On
CANNING JAR LANTERNS

Outline a darkened pathway, ornament a deck railing, or illumine the table of a midsummer's night meal with safe, flame-free, outdoor lights. My cool-to-the-touch lanterns are the simply brilliant marriage of an old fashioned canning jar and a new fangled tap-on light. Commonly available touch lights cast a cool white light from LED (light emitting diode) bulbs powered by long-lasting AAA batteries. With their gutsy beam, these little lamps light up the night even on cloudy days—something you surely can't say about most off-the-shelf solar garden lights.

The only tricky part of this project is finding a jar that will accommodate the touch light. I've had great luck with wide-mouth canning jars; the adhesive backing on the $2^3/_4$-inch light perfectly fits the standard 3-inch lids. Pint, half-pint, or quart-size—any jar will work provided it has a wide-mouth lid. Quick and easy to assemble, put up a big batch of canning jar lanterns for your next garden party.

MATERIALS

- Wide-mouth canning jars with two-part lids
- LED touch lights with adhesive backing

INSTRUCTIONS

➡ **1. Set up touch light.** Remove touch light from packaging and activate batteries by detaching protective tag according to package directions.

➡ **2. Mount touch light**. Separate canning jar lid from its accompanying ring and clean lid thoroughly to remove any oils or residue. Peel back protective paper from the adhesive disk on the bottom of the touch light, center the light on the canning jar lid, and press firmly to attach.

(continued)

Mounted touch light.

▶ **3. Finish**. Reassemble ring around the lid with the touch light in place. Tap touch light to turn on and screw assembled lid into place on the jar.

TRY THIS

A *Don't pack your lamps away at the end of summer. Line the walkway with decorative paper or plastic bag luminaria lit with canning jar lanterns and guide Halloween tricksters or Christmas carolers to the front door. No more worries about the front yard going up in flames with the first gust of wind or a soggy drizzle dampening holiday spirits.*

B *Snowbound? Using your fist, punch holes into a drift along a walkway. Place a lit canning jar lantern into the recess in the snow to illuminate your frosty ice kingdom for hours and hours.*

C *Enhance your lanterns with spray-on glass frosting. Available wherever spray paint is sold, the semi-transparent coating gently diffuses and refracts the beam cast by the touch light. Following package directions (and working outside or in a well-ventilated area to avoid breathing toxic fumes), apply spray-on glass frosting to the interior of each jar in several light, even coats until you achieve the degree of opacity desired. Prop inverted jar on a couple of chopsticks and allow the coating to dry completely before placing the lid on your finished lantern.*

Like many things in life, these little lanterns are even better with frosting.

NEST IN STYLE

Kathy Fries loves chickens almost as much as she loves plants. This botanical nest— actually a lush planting of variegated Japanese sweet flag (*Acorus gramineus* 'Ogon') crowned with an enormous glazed stoneware egg— is Kathy's homage to her colorful flock of twenty-nine chickens whose constant squawks permeate the area around their sweetly appointed coop and spacious fenced yard. In addition to bringing life and wit to the garden, the handsome birds provide the household with luscious fresh eggs, the foundation of many delicious baked goods from the kitchen.

HOMEMADE FIREFLIES

Dazzle evening garden party guests with a fanciful flight of homemade fireflies. By day the informal cluster of shepherd's crook–style hooks studded with craft magnets looks like a piece of metal garden art, echoing the rusty color of nearby plantings. But after dusk it's pure magic. I position LED (light emitting diode) bulbs and lithium coin batteries at each magnet along the hooks and fireflies appear to float above grasses and groundcovers along the edge of my front walkway.

You can purchase the metal hooks at most garden centers. Shop around for a good price on 3V lithium coin batteries which are typically required for watches, keyless locks, and small electronics; you'll save a bundle buying in bulk online or at discount electronics store. Any small craft magnet will do.

Order extra bright, white 10mm LED bulbs online; a package of fifty bulbs only set me back about twenty dollars, plus shipping. Diffused-lens bulbs cast light in every direction, while non-diffuse bulbs have a less-satisfying targeted beam. Each LED bulb has a life-span of several hundred hours; I've had bulbs that have lasted continuously for months needing only to have their battery replaced as the charge dims. Maintain the longest battery life by storing magnets separately from lithium coins to avoid prematurely draining their charge.

MATERIALS

- 36-inch metal shepherd's crook–style garden hooks
- $1/2$-inch craft magnets
- 3V CR2032 lithium coin batteries
- Extra bright, diffused-lens, white 10mm LED bulbs

INSTRUCTIONS

➡ **1. Set hooks in place.** Arrange the hooks in the garden at staggering heights, into a suitably informal but pleasing cluster. Stick a small craft magnet at the tip of each hook, adding more magnets along the shaft if you want.

(continued)

LED bulb and battery detail.

➧ 2. "Light" your fireflies. Slot a lithium coin battery between the terminals of a LED bulb placing the slightly longer terminal on the "+" side.

➧ 3. Place fireflies on hooks. Position one LED bulb and battery at each magnet, taking care to sandwich the wire terminal securely between the magnet and the battery to ensure that the bulb remains lit.

TRY THIS

A *No hooks? Attach your homemade fireflies to any garden surface that will hold a magnet like metal furniture, tools, or even hardware on a fence.*

B *Kids—of all ages—love these. Scatter homemade fireflies around a darkened bedroom and scary monsters disappear.*

C *Set the winter holidays aglow. Affix LED bulbs and batteries to wooden picks or florist wires with dark green tape and nestle into evergreen wreaths and garlands. Or discreetly weave a metal wire through mantle decorations and stud with fireflies for a magical ribbon of light without having to bother with hiding cords. A swag of fabric at the window becomes a galaxy of stars when you sandwich magnets on either side of the cloth and affix a homemade firefly to the outside magnet.*

Add some dazzle to the dusk by adhering homemade fireflies to any metal surface in the garden.

Ever-Blooming
VINYL WALLFLOWERS

This project is pure fun and totally impractical—but do it anyway for the sheer impudence of it. If you've got fifteen minutes and a stash of old records, you've already got the makings for a crop of these lighthearted vinyl wallflowers. Simply heat vinyl records—LPs or 45s—in a low-temperature oven and mold them into ruffled, petal-like forms. Affix to your fence as "singles," or double up for fuller blooms. Whether you lean toward classical, disco, or funky R&B, this is a completely fresh take on the oldies.

Those of you in the strictly digital age can find LPs and 45s at record stores carrying vintage vinyl or at garage sales and thrift stores. Trust me—ask your partner before you get into the dusty box in the basement. One person's heavy metal nightmare is another's fond adolescent artifact. Put all sort of junk drawer flotsam and stored-but-forgotten basement debris to use decorating your wallflowers. Art glass beads, spare cabinet knobs, and tiny tart tins add color and wit to this wacky garden art project.

MATERIALS

- Vinyl records, LPs or 45s
- Decorative cabinet knob with mounting bolt
- Tart tins
- Beads
- 14 and 20 gauge galvanized wire
- Bolts, nuts, and washers of varying sizes

INSTRUCTIONS

➡ **1. Heat records.** Preheat oven to 200 degrees F. Position a heat-proof glass bowl on the cookie sheet; balance record on top of the glass, centering on the label. Place cookie sheet into the oven and monitor closely as the vinyl record will begin to slump and melt after just three to five minutes in the low heat.

(continued)

Shaping heated record.

2. Mold records. Remove cookie sheet from the oven with an oven mitt for protection. Working quickly, mold and sculpt the warm vinyl with your fingers forming it into scalloped curves around the glass. While the vinyl will be warm, it will not be hot enough to burn; however, take care with the glass bowl and cookie sheet which will heat up considerably. If the vinyl cools before you are done shaping, return the set-up to the oven for a brief reheating. To make a "double" wallflower, warm both records at the same time using two glass bowls on the cookie sheet. Mold and shape both pieces together, adjusting ruffled scallops to fit. Allow records to cool completely.

3. Form wallflower hanger. Wind a 10-inch length of 14 gauge wire around a dowel twice in one direction, and then twice in the opposite, forming a figure 8–shaped hanger. Trim loose ends.

4. Assemble wall-flowers. *For knob-centered single wallflower:* Drill a hole at the center of the tiny tart tin. Thread the mounting bolt of cabinet knob through tart tin and the hole in the center of the record label. On the back side of your wallflower, position a 1 1/2-inch

Wallflower hanger detail.

washer over the protruding bolt, sandwiching one loop of a wire hanger between record and the washer. Screw on and tighten nut securing everything in place.

For double wallflower with beaded stamens: Cut two 10- to 12-inch lengths of 20 gauge wire. Fold each wire in two unequal lengths to form your beaded stamens. Thread all four cut ends with glass beads crimping the wire just below each bead; using needle-nose pliers form a tight loop at the end of each wire securing bead between crimp and loop. Wrap the center fold of each beaded wire around the head of a bolt before threading it through the center holes of two ruffled records. Position wire hanger and washer as described above, securing everything with a nut.

➡ **5. Install.** Pound nails securely into fence to hang finished wallflowers. Vary heights for a casual "naturalistic" effect.

Beading detail.

TRY THIS

A *Come down off the fence. Mount finished wallflowers to the head of a 24-inch wooden dowel and "plant" directly in the garden or a container planting.*

B *If you really must have a practical application for this whimsical project, pot up your scalloped wallflower with inky black mondo grass (Ophiopogon planiscapus 'Nigrescens') and mulch with washed black gravel. Très chic in a little-black-dress kind of way—or the perfect accessory for a gothic garden.*

AMERICANA GARDEN ART

Vertical surfaces in the garden, like fences and exterior walls, cry out for adornment and wall art. An extraordinary collection of vintage signs completely covers the face of a barn turned workshop in the garden of Johanna and Richard Marquis. The bold color and variety of forms, not to mention the stories behind these Americana artifacts of the road, infuse the garden with the personality of these two inveterate collectors. Is your unique garden persona showing?

Embellished
TERRACOTTA HOSE GUIDES

A discreet, well-placed, little garden accessory, hose guides have a big, important job: protecting plantings and helping choreograph the awkward dance between garden hose and gardener. A small stack of small terracotta pots forms the base of each hose guide, rotating and spinning on the rebar stake like a wheel on an axle. Copper, porcelain, terracotta, wood, and glass elements stack like beads over the rebar. Subtly ornamental so as not to distract from flowering beds and borders, these hose guides are tough enough to leave in place all year long.

Securely anchoring the rebar stake is the key to an effective, sturdy hose guide. If you have sandy soil as I do, opt for a longer stake and drive it deeper into the ground for a strong, fixed base. Short lengths of copper pipe (trimmed with easy-to-use pipe cutting tool made specifically for cutting copper and PVC pipe) add color and a warm glow when interspersed among other decorative elements. Both pipe and pipe cutter may be purchased in the plumbing department of hardware stores, where you're also likely to find interesting bits, knobs, and washers to embellish your hose guide. Look for wood, glass, or ceramic drapery finials and accessories at fabric stores and wherever home goods are sold.

MATERIALS

- 1 (24- or 36-inch) rebar stake, ½-inch diameter
- 2 or 3 small terracotta pots
- 24-inch length copper pipe
- Vintage glass doorknobs or art glass finial
- Decorative elements which can be threaded onto rebar (optional)

Starting materials, clockwise from bottom left: a small terracotta pot, a porcelain bathroom fixture, washers, a wooden drapery "bead," a vintage glass doorknob, the pipe cutting tool, and pieces of copper pipe.

- Rubber mallet
- Screw feed tube cutter

INSTRUCTIONS

➡ **1. Set rebar.** Pound rebar stake firmly into the ground with a rubber mallet.

➡ **2. Assemble decorative elements.** Sleeve two or three small terracotta pots over the pounded stake. If necessary, widen the pot's drainage hole by gently twisting it over the rebar until it slides freely. Using the screw feed tube cutter, cut copper pipe into 1- to 3-inch pieces. Stack copper pipe pieces and decorative elements on terracotta base, topping off your hose guide with an art glass or drapery finial.

Up close and personal with the upper portion of a decorative hose guide.

TRY THIS

- -

Put household strays to work. Add a porcelain sink fixture, large wooden drapery beads, galvanized washers, extra napkin rings, vintage glass door knobs, and miscellaneous junk drawer treasures to your stack for additional decorative impact.

OTHER GARDEN USES FOR TERRACOTTA

My collection of hundreds of small terracotta pots once belonged to a friend and next door neighbor. Gordon was a nursery man of the old-school variety; raising his stock from seeds and cuttings, patiently tending them to a marketable size. One of my earliest gardening mentors, his was an encouraging voice when I was thinking about starting my own nursery.

Gordon is gone but his beautiful horticultural legacy lives on in the many trees and shrubs that populate the large lot adjacent to ours. The property is slated for development, so I appreciate every day I still get to gaze out at the mature cedars, pines, and false cypress. Towering rhododendrons and flowering trees are overgrown with weeds and brambles, but continue to bloom year in and year out. Gordon's Garden, as it will forever be known to me, is a neighborhood treasure.

Mountains of terracotta pots from Gordon's nursery were fated for the landfill before my husband rescued them for me. The very fact that many of these pots are decades old speaks to their resourcefulness and sustainability—something which surely can not be said of the countless disposable plastic pots churned out by today's horticultural industry. Unfortunately, save for the occasional hardy succulent, I can't keep anything growing in such a small porous container. But over the years I've found other ways to put my inherited terracotta collection to work in the garden.

- Cover drainage holes in container plantings with terracotta shards to prevent the soil from washing away.
- Mark vegetable plantings by writing crop names in chalk on a large shard of terracotta or whole pot.
- Outline and define the herb garden with a row of upended terracotta pots for a casual border; or place them right side up and plant with a colorful border of chives.
- Infill nooks and crannies with stacks of mossy pots adding a decorative finishing touch to overlooked spaces that ordinarily would just spout weeds.
- Mulch pink and bronze container plantings with broken up terracotta to create a warm monochromatic color palette as you conserve soil moisture and control weeds.
- Work terracotta bits into garden mosaics and custom pavers.

FLASHING NAMEPLATES

Shiny all-weather plant markers clearly mark out rows and stylishly designate garden favorites. I'm not a huge fan of labeling everything in the garden—overzealous tagging can end up looking like a tiny graveyard studded with faded and broken nursery sticks, or an aloof, highly cataloged collection of individual plants. I'd rather focus on creating an inviting space where diverse living elements knit together into a constantly changing and dynamic environment that is much more than the sum of its parts. But sometimes you need to know where you sowed the carrots, or feel moved to christen, exhort, title, or otherwise label a part of your garden.

Easily fashioned from galvanized wire and metal flashing tiles, these durable garden markers blend beautifully and discreetly into the garden. Adorned with beads or left simple and spare, they are perfect for those occasions when you've really got something to say, or you just want to be able to tell the arugula from the spinach. Stock up for yourself and make more for friends and family.

MATERIALS

- Printer paper
- 1 (5 x 8-inch) galvanized flashing tile
- 14 and 20 gauge galvanized wire
- Glass beads

INSTRUCTIONS

➡ **1. Compose paper template.** Size your word or words to a maximum of 4 inches wide and no more than 2 inches tall, selecting a clean, sans serif font with good readability. I printed "grow," "bloom," and "herbs" in Franklin gothic book, an interesting font that is standard on most computers. Print out template(s) and cut down to fit your plant marker. Spray the backside of the template with spray mount adhesive and set aside while you complete the next step.

(continued)

▶ **2. Mark galvanized tile.** Measure and divide flashing tile into two equal 4 x 5-inch sections marking the line lightly with a pencil; this line will later form the folded top edge of your finished plant marker. My markers are two-sided for versatility; therefore each marker has two words on it. Measure and mark lines 2 inches in from each 5-inch edge; your printed word will sit on this line. Adhere paper templates in place; reverse orientation of the top word so it reads correctly once the flashing tile is folded.

A rubber mallet, a nail, and wire cutters are all you need to turn everyday galvanized wire and flashing tiles into stylish garden markers.

▶ **3. Punch letters.** With your template in place, position flashing tile on a scrap of wood. Repeatedly striking the head of a nail with rubber mallet, punch a series of closely spaced holes outlining each letter on your template. Remove paper.

▶ **4. Finish tile.** Fold flashing tile in half bending it over the edge of a table along the marked center line. Using your fingers, pinch along this beginning fold, forming an even, uniform ridge. Roll all four corners of the tile with needle-nose pliers to eliminate sharp edges.

▶ **5. Create wire holder and decorative leaf shape**. Cut a 36-inch length of 14 gauge wire. Wind one end tightly, six times, around the handle of your rubber mallet. Remove wire coil from handle and use pliers to bend remaining wire at the base of the coil into a right angle; this forms the upright "stem" of your wire holder. Cut a 10-inch length of 14 gauge wire for the leaf shape. Fold wire at 4 inches, pinching with pliers to crease; loosely coil the remaining 6-inch end. Bind leaf shape to the upright stem of your plant marker by wrapping the two together with a length of 20 gauge wire; trim ends

Glass beads fixed with glue and a few well-placed crimps on the corners of the flashing tile add finishing details to your garden marker.

neatly. Decorate wire leaf with glass beads, gluing end beads in place. Allow glue to dry.

➡ **6. Final assembly.** Pinch the folded tile and slot it into the wire coil. Tension between the spring-like coil and the folded tile holds everything in place.

TRY THIS

Don't limit yourself to simply identifying plants. A simple three word set—"be here now"—reminds us to appreciate every day in the garden. More ambitious crafters can create a series of single word markers and compose a garden bed haiku.

A giant 4-foot glass carrot (blown by Richard Marquis and crew) lords over the highly ornamental edible garden, using humor and masterful craftsmanship instead of words to declare a love of vegetables.

Put a finishing touch on the growing season with foliage, seedheads, pods, and the occasional bloom. Outside in the garden or harvested for indoor seasonal decor, the rich color and ripening fruitfulness of these plants wring every last beautiful moment from autumn's golden light before making a graceful exit into winter.

Autumn Attractions

WOODY PLANTS

American ash *(Fraxinus americana)*

Dogwood *(Cornus)*

Ginkgo *(Ginkgo)*

Katsura *(Cercidiphyllum japonicum)*

Maple *(Acer)*

Oak *(Quercus)*

Persian ironwood *(Parrotia persica)*

Smoke tree *(Cotinus coggygria)*

Sourwood *(Oxydendrum arboreum)*

Staghorn sumac *(Rhus typhina)*

American sweet gum *(Liquidambar styraciflua)*

PERENNIALS

Blackberry lily *(Belamcanda chinensis)*

Clematis *(Clematis)*

Fountain grass *(Pennisetum)*

Giant feather grass *(Stipa gigantea)*

Jerusalem sage *(Phlomis russeliana)*

Maiden grass *(Miscanthus)*

Moor grass *(Molinia)*

Purple coneflower *(Echinacea purpurea)*

Sea holly *(Eryngium)*

Sedum *(Sedum telephium)*

Switch grass *(Panicum)*

BULBS AND TUBERS

Autumn crocus *(Colchicum)*

Belladonna lily *(Amaryllis belladonna)*

Cyclamen *(Cyclamen hederifolium)*

Fall-blooming crocus *(Crocus speciosus)*

Lords and ladies *(Arum italicum 'Pictum')*

Rain lily *(Zephyranthes candida)*

ANNUALS

Big quaking grass *(Briza maxima)*

Love-in-a-mist *(Nigella damascena)*

Love-lies-bleeding *(Amaranthus caudatus)*

Milkweed *(Asclepias fruticosa)*

Pincushion flower *(Scabiosa atropurpurea)*

Poppy *(Papaver)*

Shoo-fly plant *(Nicandra physalodes)*

Spiderflower *(Cleome hassleriana)*

Sunflower *(Helianthus annuus)*

ORGANIZE & STORE

I'd rather work in the garden than keep house any day of the week, but the frenetic pace of high summer can still get the best of me as I struggle to water, weed, harvest, and tend my rather small, but intensively planted, city lot. Maintenance is the often forgotten underbelly of garden keeping and an unavoidable aspect of the care of any landscape be it a rooftop container, backyard plot, or country acre. However, the garden need not rule the gardener with a horticultural iron fist. The practical projects in this chapter will make your horticultural life easier, while still contributing flair and style to your landscape.

With the right tool at hand—and knowing

where you stored it—the battle is already half won; a wall-hung potting shed organizer keeps everyday garden necessities at the tip of your fingers. City gardeners with limited space will appreciate a low-profile planting bench that provides flexible workspace when you need it, folding out of the way when you don't. Highlighting storage and display, a shuttered column puts your favorite plant on a pedestal while conveniently stashing—or showing off—garden tools and mementos. And finally, armed with the essential tools and tips for cut flower success, you'll be ready to harvest the best of the season and bring the beauty of the garden indoors.

Open-Air
POTTING ORGANIZER

The growing season moves pretty fast. Stash everything you need to keep up with your garden's progress right at the tip of your fingers with this attractive and resourceful organizational hub. Borrowing ideas from kitchen and office wall storage systems, my potting shed organizer turns my tiny shed—really no more than an open-air storage cubby—from a tangle of tools and garden utensils into an efficient, orderly workspace.

Wooden boxes labeled by planting season help keep seeds organized for future sowing; a magnetic surface, actually a re-envisioned cookie sheet, holds to-do lists and garden notes; and cork tiles serve as a visual inspiration board and multi-layered scrapbook of the current growing season. Practical hooks, clips, and shelves ensure your favorite tools, gloves, sunscreen, and garden hat are always handy, leaving you free to consider important issues, like whether you should put in another rose or more tomatoes.

My organizer came together quickly and easily with wooden shelves from IKEA (a terrific source for well-made, inventive, and reasonably priced organizational accessories), boxes, hooks, and miscellanea left over from a variety of different indoor projects. Whether you mount your multi-tasking workstation in the potting shed, on a protected exterior wall, or indoors by the back door, you're well on your way to managing the growing season, from planning and planting through tending and harvest. Don't you feel more productive already?

MATERIALS

- 2 (12 x 35-inch) wooden shelves (GORM series, IKEA)

INSTRUCTIONS

➧ **1. Create workstation base.** Place IKEA shelves face down, side by side, aligning them along their 35-inch edge. Attach the 20-inch 1x4s, placing one at each end of the shelves, fixing the crosspieces in place with several screws. Flip base right side up so supporting crosspieces are face down.

(continued)

- 2 (20-inch) lengths 1x4 lumber
- 1 (12 x 19-inch) cookie sheet
- 2 (12 x 12-inch) cork tiles
- 3 (4½-inch) square wooden boxes
- 3 metal label holders
- 1 (11½-inch) galvanized ledge
- 1 (22-inch) towel bar
- 1 decorative hook
- 4 spring-type clothespins
- Hooks, pushpins, magnets

TOOLS & OTHER SUPPLIES

- Electric chop box or hand saw
- Screwdriver
- Hammer
- Wood screws, nails
- Heavy-duty construction adhesive
- Eye screws and braided wire for hanging

Backside detail.

2. Add features. Screw cookie sheet, galvanized tray, and decorative hook in place along the top of your workstation base. I mounted the small galvanized ledge upside down forming a shallow tray that's perfect for holding 4-inch plant starts. Fasten a double layer of cork tiles beneath the galvanized tray by nailing it in place every 4 inches around the outer edge. Mount towel bar along the bottom of the workstation base and attach vintage water faucet handle to far right side screwing it in place through the center hole

3. Attach seed sorting boxes and clothespins. Center metal label holders on wooden boxes and lightly tap prongs with a hammer, holding them in place. Insert labels that read "indoors," "spring," and "summer." Glue wooden boxes and clothespins to workstation base following construction adhesive package instructions. Allow glue to dry overnight.

4. Finish. Hang your finished potting shed organizer with sturdy eye screws and braided picture-hanging wire.

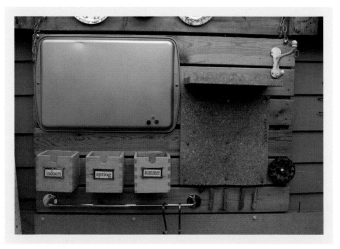

Finished organizer.

- -

A *No IKEA? Create a custom workstation base from standard 1x4 lumber. Cut six 35-inch and two 24-inch 1x4s. Lay out all six 35-inch lengths side by side spacing them ¼ inch apart forming a 24 x 35-inch backing. Position remaining 1x4s across each 24-inch end of your workstation backing. Attach crosspieces anchored with screws to every horizontal board.*

B *Mount a compact fluorescent light fixture overhead and turn your potting shed organizer into a seed-starting station.*

A WELL-APPOINTED POTTING SHED

Common kitchen and office storage accessories can help organize your garden life.

- -

- Clear, lidded plastic storage jars and containers keep garden supplies secure and dry.
- Serving trays and storage caddies sort and organize tools by task.
- Wire baskets and colanders for rinsing garden harvest keeps soil in the garden and out of the kitchen sink.
- Shallow open shelves (think spice rack) keep small containers, hose nozzles, and plant ties easily accessible.
- Task lighting brightens up your workspace on dark grey days.
- A garden "inbox" stores plant tags and care instructions.
- A wall calendar makes an easy to maintain, quick and dirty, garden journal.
- Small coin envelopes stash and store collected seeds.
- Wall-mounted, magnetic knife strip holds lightweight tools, scissors, and snips.
- Metal ruler for seed spacing and simple measures; attach to metal surface with magnets.
- Clothespins, magnets, hooks, and pegs keep things simple and visible—the more the merrier.

Easy Fold-Away
PLANTING BENCH

You can never have too many ripe tomatoes, too few weeds, or enough room to putter in the garden. My simple but sturdy, collapsible, wall-mounted planting bench eases day-to-day practical garden tasks by providing flexible workspace—right there when you need it, folding neatly out of the way when not in use. This stoop-free work area is a real boon for city gardeners where space is always at a premium; in larger gardens add another potting area or versatile work surface to any wall or fence and eliminate constant trips back to the garage or shed.

Collapsible brackets, a critical component of this project, are sold in pairs and available at custom builder's and woodworking supply stores and, of course, online. Make sure you get the heavyweight model capable of supporting hundreds of pounds and finished with a durable epoxy enamel finish that holds up to the elements. A pre-made, 12 x 35-inch wooden shelf from IKEA offers the perfect slatted surface for easy clean up, making this project no more complicated than mounting a bookshelf. See page 197 for instructions on how to build a custom shelf from standard 1x4 lumber.

Make sure to mount your fold-away planting bench to a secure, well-built surface. An extra pair of hands will help ease measuring and installation—grab an assistant and your planting bench will be ready in less than an hour.

MATERIALS

- 1 (12 x 35-inch) wooden shelf (GORM series, IKEA)
- 1 pair 12-inch heavy-duty collapsible shelf brackets and mounting hardware

INSTRUCTIONS

➡ **1. Attach brackets to shelf.** Place the top arm of each folding shelf bracket at each end of the underside of your slatted shelf. Mark and drill pilot holes before screwing brackets securely in place with accompanying mounting hardware.

(continued)

- Pencil
- Handheld power drill, ¼-inch bit
- Screwdriver
- Measuring tape
- Builder's level

➡ **2. Mount shelf.** Measure and mark the height at which your collapsible planting bench will hang on the wall or fence. A waist-high surface when standing offers the most flexibility and eases back strain. With your assistant holding the shelf in place, use your builder's level to ensure it hangs evenly. Mark and drill pilot holes for the remaining mounting screws through the back brackets before mounting your folding planting bench securely in place.

Folding shelf bracket detail.

TRY THIS

Ⓐ *Complete your flexible planting station with potting soil stored in a handsome, galvanized garbage can. A wall-hung blackboard with an attached shelf keeps clippers and seed packets handy and reminds you when it's time to plant.*

Ⓑ *A back porch fold-away planting bench is also a perfect surface for outdoor entertaining. Use the extra space to serve up drinks or furnish a barbeque workstation—stash charcoal briquettes in the garbage can and list the evening's menu on the blackboard.*

IF THESE WALLS COALD TALK

What do your garden walls say about you? I've put my "walls"—actually just an old cedar fence—to work. Mounted wooden nursery flats hold pots of veggie starts awaiting placement in the garden. An old wire milk crate has been transformed into cubby featuring a favorite potted plant and a Japanese fishing float. I love anything sea foam green, maybe it's that seashore thing again. Displaying odd bits and pieces united by a single color elevates clutter to a collection; putting it on my working wall keeps it from getting in the way of real garden work. The chicken? I keep threatening to get chickens—but all I really want are the eggs.

Repurposed
SHUTTER STORAGE SPACE

Is it a plant stand with storage or a versatile shelf unit that puts your favorite potted plant on a pedestal? A pair of hinged shutters joined into a distinctive architectural column is a handsome display piece with a heart of hardworking storage. A slate tile top provides a beautiful, all-weather perch for plants while interior shelves hold extra gardening gloves, plant ties, and small tools, saving you a trip to the tool shed while tending entryway or back porch containers. There's even a place to stash muddy boots or gardening clogs—one small step toward keeping garden dirt outside where it belongs.

Shutters may be found at salvage yards or purchased new at a lumber yard or full service hardware store. The following directions are specific to working with recycled shutters that are each $4\frac{1}{2}$ feet tall by 1 foot wide. When working with repurposed goods, measure and cut fitted elements, like the interior shelves and supporting cleats in this project, as you go. This allows you to make slight adjustments for uneven angles and other factors of age. The extra effort will save you having to redo a step and any inconsistencies merely contribute to the unique charm of your finished piece.

Other lumber in this project is standard and may be purchased—and often pre-cut—at your local hardware store or lumber yard. Porcelain cabinet knobs functioning as ball feet keep the base of the shelf unit elevated and dry even in exposed conditions.

MATERIALS

- 2 matching pairs of hinged shutters; mine are $4\frac{1}{2}$ feet tall x 1 foot wide

INSTRUCTIONS

➡ **1. Assemble column.** Determine which shutter will be the front door of your finished shelf unit. Remove extra hardware, leaving only the front door shutter still on its hinges. Position remaining shutters to form a four-sided box with the operable door facing forward. If your shutter's louvers are fixed, make sure they are pointing in the same direction. Secure fixed sides with right-angled metal fastener plates screwed into place at the top and bottom in each back corner.

(continued)

- 4 right-angled metal fastener plates
- 1 (6-foot) length 1x8 lumber, cut into 4 (16-inch) pieces
- 4 (2-inch) porcelain cabinet knobs with mounting bolts
- 2 (7 foot x 1-inch) lengths screen molding or ¼-inch lath
- 2 (11 x 12-inch) pieces ¼-inch plywood (adjusted to fit interior dimensions)
- 2 (12 x 12-inch) sheets 1-inch mosaic slate tiles
- Pre-mixed grout, dark grey to match slate tile

TOOLS & OTHER SUPPLIES

- Screwdriver
- Mounting screws
- Handheld power drill, ⅛-inch bit
- Circular saw or hand saw
- Tin snips
- Heavy-duty construction adhesive
- Sponge

2. Construct top and base.

Position two 16-inch lengths of 1x8 lumber and screw into place forming the base of your shelf unit. Mount the four porcelain knobs to the outside bottom of the shelf unit; drill pilot holes and screw into place with the mounting hardware that came with the knobs, working from inside the cabinet frame. Form the top of your shelf unit with the remaining two lengths of 1x8 lumber and screw into place as you did on the base.

3. Install interior shelves.

Cut screen molding or lath strips into two supporting cleats for each plywood shelf. I cut 11-inch cleats to fit the 12-inch wide shutters. Recessing the shelves allows clearance for the door of the cabinet to open and close. Drill pilot holes at the end of each shelf cleat. Carefully measure down from the top of the cabinet so each shelf sits level and mark cleat positions. Screw supporting cleats into place and position shelves.

Base with cabinet knob feet.

Corner fastening and shelf supporting cleat detail.

4. Affix tile top. Trimming mesh between tiles with tin snips, cut and arrange mosaic slate tiles to cover a 14 x 16-inch area. Apply heavy-duty construction adhesive to the back of each tile section and glue tiles to the top surface of your shutter shelf cabinet. Weight the glued surface and leave to dry for at least 24 hours before grouting.

5. Grout tile. Apply pre-mixed grout according to package instructions, carefully working it into all the joints and crevices around each individual 1-inch tile. Using a damp sponge, remove extra grout and clean the surface of the tiles before the grout begins to set.

6. Finish. Screw short lengths of leftover screen molding or wooden lath around the top tiled surface to finish off raw edges.

Grouting tile top.

TRY THIS

A *Sturdy hooks easily fit over shutter louvers keeping garden snips and a small container for seeds handy. Scrap linoleum tiles lend color and durability to finished shelves.*

B *Grill masters can turn shutter shelf columns into an outdoor pantry stocked with barbeque utensils and accessories.*

Cut Flower
BOUQUET 101

Easily distinguished from anonymous dial-up arrangements or cello-wrapped grocery store bunches, handmade flower bouquets celebrate the color, fragrance, and exact moment of the season in your own backyard. Creating fresh garden bouquets is a breeze when you've gathered everything necessary to harvest, arrange, and care for your seasonal bounty in one convenient location. An old metal tool box is a great place to store an assortment of basic garden and household clippers, knives, and tools, along with a few unexpected kitchen cupboard staples. For ultimate cut flower success, make sure to stay vigilant toward the one thing that cannot be held in your tool box—fresh, clean water. Once you've assembled all the essential tools, just follow this quick guide to processing cut flowers for the longest vase life.

MATERIALS

- An assortment of flowers (see "Garden Plants for Cutting")
- Metal tool box
- Sharp knife
- Bypass pruners
- Floral snips
- Pruning saw
- Hammer
- Chicken wire
- Twine or raffia
- Flower freshener

INSTRUCTIONS

▶ **1. Harvest.** Cut tender green stems with a sharp knife, bypass pruners, or floral snips. Angled cuts yield a larger cut surface and increased water absorption. Avoid dull blades and anvil-style tools which pinch plant cells closed, damaging their ability to take up water. It's best to harvest flowers in the morning before the heat of the day has sapped plant moisture.

▶ **2. Prepare.** Strip extra foliage and any thorns from cut stems to concentrate water to the flowers. Also remove any leaves falling below the water level to prevent decay. Crush woody stems by smashing their ends with a hammer or scraping away the bottom couple of inches of bark, allowing them to drink freely. Stems that emit a sticky sap, like euphorbias, poppies, acanthus, and hellebores,

(continued)

☐ Bucket

☐ Vase

require an additional step: hold sappy stems over a gas flame on the stove or a lit candle to cauterize and seal cut ends.

▶ **3. Condition.** Plunge prepared stems immediately into a bucket of deep tepid water allowing them to rest in a cool dark spot for one to several hours. (Getting cut stems into water as quickly as possible prevents air bubbles from blocking exposed water channels.) This conditioning step ensures cut flowers are completely hydrated, which makes them easier to arrange and extends the life of your finished bouquet.

▶ **4. Arrange.** Fill scrupulously clean vase with water and flower freshener and arrange conditioned flowers. A scrap of crumpled chicken wire tucked into an opaque container helps anchor stems in vase arrangements; tie hand-held bouquets with twine or raffia.

▶ **5. Care.** Nothing shortens the life of cut flowers faster than decay. Freshening or replacing vase water daily and keeping bouquets out of direct sunlight helps maintain a clean, healthy environment. If flowers wilt, revive by trimming cut ends and completely submerging in a bathtub filled with cool water.

Vase water additives further extend the life of your arrangement by providing sugars for plant growth and inhibiting bacterial growth. Purchase commercial additives from florists, craft stores, and even the corner grocery, or experiment with making your own flower freshener using common kitchen staples. Here are a few simple recipes to try:

A *Dissolve 1 tablespoon of sugar in 1 quart of warm water along with 2 tablespoons of lemon juice and $1/2$ teaspoon of bleach.*

B *Combine 1 cup lemon-lime soda (not diet) with 3 cups water and $1/4$ teaspoon bleach.*

C *A shot of vodka (don't waste the good stuff) in vase water fights bacterial growth while sugars in the alcohol support the plant.*

D *Traditional floral folklore recommends acidulating water with aspirin or adding a few copper pennies for their antifungal properties; however, pennies dated 1983 and later are mostly zinc with a thin copper coating—not enough to be effective.*

Harvesting plants for the vase is a natural extension of the garden itself. With a little planning and some imagination, even a small city-sized yard filled with woody shrubs, hardy perennials, bulbs, and seasonal annuals can yield abundant material for fresh cut bouquets throughout the year. Don't forget to look beyond the bloom: richly colored leaves, interesting bark, seed heads, and fruits or berries add texture and personality to your finished arrangements.

Garden Plants for Cutting

WOODY PLANTS

Flowering quince *(Chaenomeles)*

Hydrangea *(Hydrangea)*

Lavender *(Lavandula)*

Lilac *(Syringa)*

Mexican orange *(Choisya ternata)*

Red twig dogwood *(Cornus sanguinea)*

Rose *(Rosa)*

Smoke tree *(Cotinus coggygria)*

Winter daphne *(Daphne odora)*

PERENNIALS

Black-eyed Susan *(Rudbeckia)*

Bleeding heart *(Dicentra)*

Brazilian verbena *(Verbena bonariensis)*

Delphinium *(Delphinium)*

Foxglove *(Digitalis)*

Lily of the valley *(Convallaria majalis)*

Peony *(Paeonia)*

Peruvian lily *(Alstroemeria)*

Wallflower *(Erysimum)*

BULBS, CORMS, AND TUBERS

Daffodil *(Narcissus)*

Dahlia *(Dahlia)*

Gladiolus *(Gladiolus)*

Hyacinth *(Hyacinthus)*

Iris *(Iris)*

Lily *(Lilium)*

Montbretia *(Crocosmia)*

Ornamental onion *(Allium)*

Tulip *(Tulipa)*

ANNUALS

Bachelor's button *(Centaurea cyanus)*

Bells of Ireland *(Moluccella laevis)*

Cosmos *(Cosmos)*

Larkspur *(Consolida ajacis)*

Love-in-a-mist *(Nigella damascena)*

Pot marigold *(Calendula officinalis)*

Snapdragon *(Antirrhinum majus)*

Sunflower *(Helianthus annuus)*

Sweet pea *(Lathyrus odoratus)*

Zinnia *(Zinnia)*

CONVERSION TABLES

INCHES / CENTIMETERS

1/8	=	0.3	7	=	18
1/4	=	0.6	8	=	20
3/8	=	0.9	9	=	23
1/2	=	1.25	10	=	25
5/8	=	1.6	12	=	30
3/4	=	1.9	15	=	38
1	=	2.5	18	=	45
1 1/2	=	3.8	20	=	50
2	=	5.0	24	=	60
3	=	7.5	30	=	75
4	=	10	32	=	80
5	=	12.5	36	=	90
6	=	15	60	=	150

FEET / METERS

1/4	=	0.08	8	=	2.4
1/3	=	0.1	9	=	2.7
1/2	=	0.15	10	=	3.0
1	=	0.3	12	=	3.6
1 1/2	=	0.5	15	=	4.5
2	=	0.6	20	=	6.0
2 1/2	=	0.8	25	=	7.5
3	=	0.9	30	=	9.0
4	=	1.2	35	=	10.5
5	=	1.5	40	=	12
6	=	1.8	45	=	13.5
7	=	2.1	50	=	15

TEMPERATURES

$$°C = \tfrac{5}{9} \times (°F-32)$$

$$°F = (\tfrac{9}{5} \times °C) + 32$$

AVERAGE ANNUAL MINIMUM TEMPERATURE

ZONE	TEMPERATURE (DEG. F)	TEMPERATURE (DEG. C)
1	Below –50	Below –46
2	–50 to –40	– 46 to –40
3	–40 to –30	– 40 to –34
4	–30 to –20	– 34 to –29
5	–20 to –10	– 29 to –23
6	–10 to 0	– 23 to –18
7	0 to 10	– 18 to –12
8	10 to 20	– 12 to –7
9	20 to 30	– 7 to –1
10	30 to 40	– 1 to 4
11	40 and above	4 and above

To see the U.S. Department of Agriculture Hardiness Zone Map, go to the U.S. National Arboretum site at http://www.usna.usda.gov/Hardzone/ushzmap.html.

RESOURCES

Materials for the projects in this book are easily purchased, obtained, or salvaged. Heck, you may discover some already in your basement. Search beyond expected retailers and sources within the garden industry to local thrift stores, independent Mom-and-Pop establishments, artist supply stores, and estate sales (hint: the good stuff's in the garage). An online search will turn up local resources and retail outlets for recycled and salvaged materials. Try keywords: used building materials, surplus lumber, scrap metal, architectural salvage. And don't forget about the abandoned treasures just waiting to be picked up curbside; that's where I snagged my cast iron bathtub.

Ideas and inspiration are everywhere and awareness is the garden crafter's sharpest tool. I find myself going back, again and again, to a handful of seriously muse-worthy websites: www.anthropologie.com (a chain retailer with the heart and soul of handmade craft and beautiful living); www.designspongeonline.com (a daily website celebrating good design, DIY resourcefulness, and stylish living); and www.etsy.com (an online marketplace for buying and selling handmade goods and a bonanza of inspiring ideas and images).

A profoundly valuable resource for gardeners beginning and expert alike is the knowledgeable advice obtained at your local nursery, Master Gardeners chapter, horticultural society, garden club, or even your neighbor next door. Gardeners love to talk gardening and tend to be generous with helpful tips, shared plants and, if you're lucky, an abundant harvest. Nurseries and garden centers—our link between the world of horticultural bounty and the path to success in our own backyards—are where you can find plants, floral supplies, containers, quality organic potting mix, bamboo poles, terracotta, mulch, fountain pumps, peat moss or coco coir, and copper slug barrier. The real value of any nursery, large or small, is the people behind the plants; nursery workers are a wealth of information and expert in the possibilities and challenges of local gardening conditions.

Here are some suppliers of specific materials, as well as more general information, that I relied on to create the projects in this book:

AMERICAN BOXWOOD SOCIETY
www.boxwoodsociety.org

A great resource for more information on taking boxwood cuttings.

CONCRETE DEPOT
www.concretedepot.net

A comprehensive source for cement tools, equipment, colorants and stains, and Fibermesh.

CRAIGSLIST
www.craigslist.org

Online classified listings and forums, searchable by community. This is where I found my vintage trailer.

Unlock the potential in everyday materials. Garden of Sylvia Matlock and Ross Johnson.

EVIL MAD SCIENCE

www.evilmadscience.com

Online resource for 10mm LED bulbs.

GORILLA GLUE

www.gorillaglue.com

My favorite all-purpose, heavy-duty construction adhesive.

HOME DEPOT

www.homedepot.com

Hardware stores located throughout North America which stock lumber, galvanized wire, fencing, tools, heavy-duty construction adhesive, zip ties, Portland cement, concrete mix, plumbing pipes, builder's sand, wire, cement colorant, copper pipes, canning jars, vinyl tubing, galvanized gutters, copper termite flashing, rope, and chain.

IKEA

www.ikea.com

A worldwide resource for household and organizational supplies, shelving, lighting fixtures, lithium coin batteries, hooks, and decorative finials.

KRYLON

www.krylon.com

A resource for water-based landscape marking chalk.

LAWNSCAPES: MOWING PATTERNS TO MAKE YOUR YARD A WORK OF ART

A book by David Parfitt (Quirk books, 2007).

MICHAELS

www.michaels.com

Craft supplier of wire, craft magnets, decorative beads, and copper sheets. Locations throughout the United States and Canada.

RE-STORE

www.re-store.org

Resale outlets for reusable and surplus building materials, furniture, home accessories, and appliances, located throughout the United States and Canada. Proceeds help local Habitat for Humanity affiliates fund construction of Habitat homes within their communities.

REUSABLE BUILDING MATERIALS EXCHANGE (RBME)

An online database offering reusable building materials for little or no money. Check your local .gov website for participation.

TRUE VALUE

www.truevalue.com

Neighborhood-based network of over 5,000 retailer-owned hardware stores.

WOODCRAFT

www.woodcraft.com

Resource for folding shelf brackets.

The well-loved garden journal of Johanna and Richard Marquis dates back nearly twenty years. Documenting seed purchases, pest cycles, beloved blooms, proven garden shortcuts, seasonal to-do lists, and an ongoing glossary of favorite garden terms, it has become one of their most valuable tools.

INDEX

About the Author

Lorene Edwards Forkner lives, gardens, writes, and designs in the Pacific Northwest. Lorene is the coauthor of three previous books: *Hortus Miscellaneous, Growing Your Own Vegetables,* and *Canning and Preserving Your Own Harvest*. Her writing has also appeared in several national and regional publications including *Organic Gardening, MaryJane's Farm, Pacific Horticulture, Northwest Garden News,* and *Edible Seattle*. Lorene is an active speaker and teacher on topics that range from messy mudpie hypertufa to creating gardens that feed both body and spirit. Lorene's website is www.plantedathome.com, where she regularly blogs about life, work, home, and garden.